SOUTHWEST
SAGE
ANTHOLOGY

Presented by
SouthWest Writers

SouthWest Writers
Carlisle Executive Offices
3200 Carlisle Blvd N.E.
Albuquerque, New Mexico 87110
www.southwestwriters.com

SouthWest Sage Anthology, Rose Marie Kern, Editor

What is the *Sage*?

The motto of SouthWest Writers is "Writers Helping Writers." We do this through classes, conferences, workshops and a membership of more than 350 people—many of whom are published, well-known authors—who network with each other. The *SouthWest Sage* newsletter is not just a report of what is going on in the organization; it is an avenue by which authors receive good information relating to the craft of writing and through which our members can sharpen their skills.

Each month the *Sage* offers our members a challenge, an opportunity to submit their work. The editor of the *Sage* reviews the submissions and works with the individuals to refine their stories, articles, poems or essays prior to publication. Challenges reach out to all genres, encouraging the members to put pen to paper and share their talents. They may simply be a specific genre, a holiday story, or a memoir, or the challenge may be a phrase or idea. The first challenge was to write an article completing the following sentence:

"(subject): Cheaper Than Therapy"

These challenges give our members insight into the editing and critiquing processes necessary to being accepted by larger publications.

In addition to being educational, SWW meetings and workshops frequently result in stories or poems being created by the attendees. The conferences tend to stimulate new creations as well.

Many successful SouthWest Writers members contribute their time and effort to helping others by sending articles to the *Sage* aimed at providing insights into the world of writing, editing, and publishing. This includes marketing techniques, debates on traditional publishing versus self-publishing, and legal issues such as copyrights and inheritance decisions.

Sections in the book relate to SWW events which inspired stories and articles: meetings, workshops, classes and conferences. There are also pieces which were created by members/authors from their own unbound imaginations and sent for us to enjoy.

Frequently the meeting on the first Saturday of the month is followed by a writing workshop offering hands-on training. The presenters may follow the workshop with an article in the *Sage* which complements their workshop, or the attendees may write pieces during the workshop and submit them to the *Sage* for possible publication.

No one who writes for the *SouthWest Sage* is compensated with anything other than personal satisfaction and the ability to say they have been published. Yet, the items published in this local newsletter stand up to any in the nation. The *SouthWest Sage* has won awards from the New Mexico Press Women's Association for the last two years.

The *SouthWest Sage* newsletter reaches an international audience with thousands of hits each month. It is downloaded from our website www.southwestwriters.com. This book is a compilation of the best articles, stories, poems and essays from the years 2016 through 2018.

Credits

SouthWest Writers is fortunate to have hundreds of members who are not only published authors but also editors, photographers, proofreaders and formatters. The following members contributed these skills to the production of the 2018 *Sage Anthology*.

Cover, Interior Design and Layout by Rose Marie Kern

Front Cover Photograph donated by Jasmine Tritten

Proofreaders:
>   Don DeNoon
>   Stan Rhine
>   Sarah Baker

Interior Photographs by Joanne Bodin and Rose Marie Kern

Interior Artwork by Joanne Bodin

Contents

Preface by Sarah H. Baker, SWW President

Sage Challenge: Beginnings

Poetry

Writers Unbound

Sage Advice: Articles about Writing

Sage Authors' Information Section

*Anonymous published author

Preface

BY SARAH H. BAKER,
PRESIDENT SOUTHWEST WRITERS

In the early 1980s, a group of five New Mexico romance writers formed the New Mexico Romance Writers (NMRW). This group met in living rooms and talked about writing romance. They hosted their first conference in 1983 and added a writing contest to the 1984 conference. By 1985, NMRW had grown to 150 members; the group changed its name to Southwest Writers Workshop (SWW) to include writers of all genres. In 1989, SWW incorporated as a non-profit corporation. (For more information on the group's history, read *An Abridged History of SouthWest Writers* by Larry Greenly, available by link from SWW's "About" webpage.)

SouthWest Writers, as it is now known, is a vital, evolving group of writers from all walks of life and every step along the writing path. We have well-published authors who willingly share information with those who are pre-published. We have writers of novels, non-fiction, picture books, short stories, articles, screenplays, plays, and songs. And we have members who willingly volunteer their time to help others hone their writing skills and better understand the world of publishing.

Long before I joined SWW, I directed writers to the group. I'd attended a few meetings and was impressed by the friendly, welcoming membership. As soon as I moved to Albuquerque, I signed up. Even as a published author, I'm inspired by every speaker and learn something new every month. At the beginning of each meeting, members share successes so we can celebrate with them. They also share information to help others discover new opportunities. This truly is a group of writers helping writers; I encourage you to join us if you haven't already.

Although many of us know each other from SWW meetings, we are not necessarily familiar with each other's writing. The Sage Anthology offers a unique opportunity for us to read our members' work and discover new favorite authors. Enjoy!

SAGE CHALLENGE:
BEGINNINGS

It is appropriate that the stories submitted for the January issue of the *Sage* should be centered on beginnings. They range from the pain of a young woman escaping an agonizing life, to the confusion of someone in a new job, to the complex decision to whether a person can handle adopting a pet.

Sometimes we build walls or burn bridges when we leave our old life and move on to a new one. Or walls are placed in our minds by accidents and injuries, so when we open our eyes everything is new. Anyone who aspires to be an author will be able to relate to the moment they sit down and write the first line of a story.

NIGHT RIDE

BY S.A. MONTOYA GALLEGOS

Night folded around her like a cocoon. If not for the occasional dip in the road, Julia felt she was aboard a spaceship instead of racing through the New Mexico mountains in her 1976 Chevy Monte Carlo.

Inside the cabin of the car, the eerie glow of the dashboard cast a greenish tint on the white bench seat. Outside, the speed of the car made the road lines connect ahead of the long nose of the vehicle. Pine trees occasionally streaked by—elongated black and brown lines, vaguely suggesting a world outside.

Julia took a deep breath, and the scent of her two children sleeping on the back seat wafted up to her. Julia never felt she had an inborn maternal instinct. She looked at her children as distinct individuals brought to her by fate. Still, Julia loved them at the most organic, atomic level. Cristina, who was now seven and very independent, generally resisted her mother's caress, but Ricardo, at three, still enjoyed the tickles that allowed Julia to breathe in the sweet-salty sweat, milk and juvenile mammal scent. It was comforting, and it gave Julia a tingle in the pit of her stomach.

As she thought about the kids and her future, Julia struggled to keep her tears at bay. She left her hometown hours before, feeling rushed and not in control. She hated that. As a schoolteacher and throughout her life, she had situations thrust on her, having to respond to events that were not created by her, but having to make things right to feel safe.

Like the day she found her mother dead, lying on the kitchen floor, her head split open with an iron skillet. It seemed like an eternity, but it was only a week ago. So much had happened since. Daniel, her husband, a drug addict and womanizer, had warned her not to tell police. It was an accident, he said. Just the same, he thrust her against the wall and knocked some sense into her, telling her he'd be back—if she was lucky. Shaggy haired and bearded, a long mustache dragging his mouth into a surly snicker, Daniel attempted a kiss. Julia shuddered and turned her head. This was the last time, she swore.

Without letting the kids know, in the midst of her mother's funeral, she spent the week frantically calling longtime friends in Colorado to secure a hiding place for her and the children. A college acquaintance, a friend said, has a farmhouse in Animas. Would that do?

Now, her getaway plan was in motion. Four, five hours passed. A few lights twinkled about a mile down the road, as she cleared the pines and the road opened up to the village. She slowed the car to see what this new world looked like, and as the road curved, the headlights illuminated the place—cottonwoods at the gate and a ranch house about a quarter mile down the road, almost hidden from view.

The wind gusted through the trees and across her face as she left the car, closing the door slowly so as not to wake her precious cargo. Julia thrust the key in the lock and slowly turned the knob. The light switch didn't work. She surveyed the room with the flashlight--gold shag carpet of unknown age, smelling of dust and pets and no curtains on the two large picture windows.

Julia was glad she had brought several blankets and sleeping bags. Tonight, we camp, she declared to herself. Hauling the sleeping bags in, she laid them under the window near the door, where the wind was least strong—and if necessary, they could escape an attacker by being close to the door, she reasoned.

"Wake up, Cristina," she whispered to her oldest in the back seat. "We're here." She walked the sleepy child up the steps and into the house with the blanket still wrapped around the girl. Julia guided Cristina onto her place closest to the wall on top of the bag. "Sweet dreams," she whispered with a kiss. Cristina nuzzled her mother and coiled herself into a ball.

Julia went back for Ricardo, a tiny bundle of clothes and blankets. Waking just enough to remember his stuffed rabbit, Ricardo mumbled, "Don't forget Peter." Julia fumbled around the car seat and found the stuffed treasure, placing it on top of his chest and carrying him inside.

As she lay next to the children, Julia focused on the starlit sky through the dusty window. Normally, the stars made her feel connected to the universe, but tonight they looked like a thousand intruders' eyes. Even so, we're safe for now, she thought, closing her eyes. Tomorrow's a new day.

FIRST FISH

BY DR. RICHARD PECK

The river on the small farm next to our 20 acres had two ends. One end butted up against our onion patch.

The other reached south to nourish the clump of burdock beside the Steiners' driveway. Slick water in the river – only three feet deep -- was a tarnished mirror where the sweep of passing clouds painted apparent ripples.

"It's just a muddy ditch," my dad said. "Not a river. And no fish. Stay away from it."

"There's crawfish in the banks."

"Uh huh. And you can drown if you fall in."

No sense arguing. I sat on the back porch and waited. Wind pushed the clouds into white piles east beyond the river.

When Dad drove to town after lunch, I went fishing.

Every few feet along the riverbank were puncture holes, each ringed with black raisin mud balls. The crawfish push out the little balls when they dig headfirst into the mud.

Reach in and grab the crawfish, throw away his pinchers and bait your hook with the curved tail. Fish can't resist the twitching bait, people say.

Then my mother stood ankle-deep in the onions, calling me.

"What about the fish?"

"No fish! You come on home, now."

I dropped the pole on the muddy bank. "I can't!" I shouted, running to meet her. "I got a bite! Really!"

It was the first time I lied to her. I was ten.

She held up both hands, a dirty trowel in one, a clump of onions in the other. Her hair was mussed by the wind. "Your dad said you stay out of there!"

"Please, Ma! I got a bite, really. Let me get my fish!"

She looked at me a long moment, before she nodded. "Then you come home."

I ran back but my pole was gone!

Not on the muddy bank. Not in the weeds. Then I saw it bobbing in the water, like a stiff eel, swimming through the parentheses of ripples. I jumped in, water waist-deep and cold and stinking like rotten apples.

A bullhead was towing the fishpole. A whiskered bullhead near a foot long, weighed maybe a pound, the baited hook swallowed belly deep.

I carried the bullhead, slippery in my fist, into our yard where it flopped clear, and I had to grab it slimy off the grass, dropped the pole and tripped over it, still running to the house, where I slipped the bullhead into the downspout-fed rain barrel.

Dad would come home soon.

I'd lied to my mother but the lie came true, so that was okay. Proof was swimming in the rain barrel.

When Dad got home I told them both the whole truth. My dad was mad at first, and then he wasn't. We went to fetch the fish from the rain barrel.

It wasn't there. Nor on the grass.

They didn't believe me. No matter how I told it. Mom had believed my lie. Neither one believed the truth.

Ever.

I stopped telling the story.

Someday I may know what it meant.

TRIXIE'S FIRST DAY

BY R. J. MIRABAL

The shaft of sunlight pouring through the unshuttered window covered the dozing brown dog in a blanket of warmth, welcome in the bare concrete viewing room. She yawned, allowing her eyes to open slightly. There were two humans looking at her!

Through the large windows she saw an older couple. Their voices sounded kind, not the barking voice of the only owner she had known until a month ago. They spoke something now familiar for the last few weeks: "Mamasita."

"Mamasita"? Must be what those in this building full of lost animals called her. All her life the barking man called her, "Bandit." None of this made sense. What mattered was that she needed a new owner. She had enough of this place of concrete walls and the smell of too many strangers.

The dog stood, stretched front and back. A sharp pain shot across her tummy. Something odd had happened days earlier when she was sent into a room of foul chemical odors. They put her into an unnatural sleep. Awakening, she felt pain in her groin and was shackled into a horrid plastic funnel surrounding her face making it hard to reach her beloved food pan.

In spite of her groggy head, sore tummy, and damnable funnel, she approached the door to regard the couple who seemed very interested in her. She noted the lack of dog hair on their pants. They might not have any other pets.

She was ready for a new home after spending her three years of life in a house of 25 other dogs, eight of them her own puppies born a couple of months before. Invaders had cruelly removed her, her puppies, and most of her other companions, carting them away in vans filled with smelly wire cages. The van was a horror of pitching motions, frantic barks and cries. They ended up in this concrete building surrounded by strange people, dogs, and cats.

Now, puppies gone, her maternal instinct thwarted and growing dormant by the day, she only wanted release from this shelter to seek the natural freedom meant for dogs. A captive all her life, she only knew the stifling house—smelling more dog than human—the big backyard of barren dirt with little in the way of tasty grass or holes promising of gophers and rabbits. Of course, she knew nothing of such beasts, but something inside told her she was missing out.

For days, in the viewing room, she saw parades of big and little humans—noisy, pointing, making sounds that hurt her ears even through the thick glass. But now this couple murmured quietly. Pleasant voices that seemed to appreciate her in spite of her swollen mammary glands still full for her absconded pups.

She wagged her tail and engaged them in the one way that would always please her old barking owner: she looked deeply and longingly into their eyes.

They were hooked.

Or were they? They moved on. Watching with expectation for a few minutes, she sighed with a low grunt and returned to her spot on the concrete bench still warm from the sunlight. Several minutes later, one of the young humans came in and clicked a leash on her collar.

Her daily walk. Great!

But no, this was different. The young one took her to the yards outside. And there was the older couple greeting her with laughing sounds, cooing gently as they petted her. She allowed them to touch her, but still wary of strangers up this close, she wandered about the fenced yard and explored the multitude of scents her fellow prisoners left on the ground and chain-link fence. She added a pile of her own scent and then sauntered back to the couple.

They still seemed interested in her saying the "Mamasita" sound. Too soon, the male human left and brought back the young one. The humans exchanged sounds that seemed pleasant enough, but then the couple left.

Damn. Oh well.

Next day, waiting for the afternoon sun to shine through the window, the brown dog was startled awake. The older couple had returned, elated while pointing at her and calling her closer to the door. She trotted over. More smiles.

They left for a while, but soon returned and entered with the young human. This time, they were making welcoming sounds and saying over and over a new word: "Trixie."

What was that? No matter. They took her outside, walked her across the parking lot, and loaded her into their car. It wasn't like that van of horror, but it was still a little scary.

However, looking out the window as they left, she felt it was different this time.

This was Trixie's first day.

AWAKENING

BY YVONNE WILLIAMS CASAUS

The light was so bright; I strained to open my eyes. I thought. *Is this heaven?* The glow all around me was blinding. A snowflake landed on my eyelash. As I strained to look down I saw a giant rock, more like a boulder on me.

I started screaming. Footsteps came crunching through the snow. A flushed face gasped, "oh my God!" I couldn't move. I began to panic; my body was frozen like ice. Another teenage girl appeared. Somehow they got the giant boulder off of me. Before the world started spinning I saw the car teetering over me.

I strained to open my eyes. The sky glowed nearly orange, from the sparkling snow on the ground. *I must have blacked out.* I tried to sit up, but two kind green eyes came into view.

A voice gently said, "You've been in an accident." He took a deep breath, "your friends went to get help, try not to move". With calm affect he added, "Don't try to move, I don't know how badly you're injured". I thought I should panic, yet somehow I felt safe. It was nearly euphoric.

He continued, "It was snowing pretty hard, it might take a minute. Your car spun on the bridge." His eyes widened, "it's amazing what adrenaline can do. Your friends got that gigantic boulder off of you."

"I am sure your friends are okay", he said to convince himself more than me; "they went with a trucker for help. I offered to stay in case you woke up." With hesitation he added, "I didn't want your friend to go with the trucker alone. I thought they'd be safer together".

Am I dreaming? I thought, and then memories started flooding me. I had fought with my mom, I had tried to beat curfew. There were sirens, then the roar of a diesel. I turned towards my new friend, my guardian angel. As I lifted my head, it throbbed unbearably. Then the world went black again.

I heard beeping. I fought to open my heavy eyes. A shadow, then a face started to form. "She's awake!" I tried to focus on the face and the familiar voice. "Oh Thank God!" My mom started kissing and hugging me. "I'm so glad you are okay!" I remembered our fight, the screaming and yelling, the mean things I said. "Oh mom, I am so sorry." I said sheepishly, "I didn't mean what I said, I love you so much".

Tears poured from her eyes, "Oh honey, I know. I love you. Always know how much I love you. I am so grateful you are okay."

"The car!" I started to panic.

She shushed me, "cars can be replaced. You cannot." She continued, "You truly are protected by angels." She looked at me sternly, "Listen to me. You have been given a second chance. There is no way you should be sitting here in this bed with only a broken arm and a bruised leg." She looked up towards the ceiling, "God must have great plans for you."

Green eyes! My guardian angel popped in my mind. "Mom, what about that guy that waited with me?" She looked at me with concern, "I'm not sure sweetheart. We got there after the ambulance. Did someone wait with you?"

"Well, now I'm not sure... maybe I dreamed it." Those eyes stayed in the back of my mind. My friends later said someone offered to stay with me while they went looking for help. In the chaos they didn't remember his name. He left when the ambulance arrived. I was disappointed, but there was nothing I could do.

A few weeks later, I went back to high school. I had a new determination. I no longer wanted to skate through my classes. This accident was a wake-up call. I had a second chance at life. As the snow melted, I connected with the new blossoms breaking through the hard ground. Like the seeds sprouting with new life and purpose, I grew and embraced the future. I no longer feared it. My Mom was right. Surviving that night was a miracle. I had another chance. I could not waste it. I had to live purposely.

The rest of the year I really focused on my schoolwork. I got straight A's for the first time in my life. One day in a small bookstore, I turned quickly and knocked a book out of a handsome young man's hands. I picked up the book with embarrassment and glanced up into his eyes. My breath caught in my throat, my heart skipped a beat. It was him. *Green eyes!* I nearly yelled, but no words would come out. He smiled, I felt butterflies. "It's you," we said in unison.

MINUTE, WRITING CLASS

BY RAYMOND C. MOCK

The class began with Marsha reading two articles on the semicolon. First, she read the blunt-fisted assault on it, and then the artfully endearing praise. I was glad to have heard both.

Next, Dennis conducted his reading and discussion of professional verse. But despite my comment, I noticed I was laid-back. It seemed I'd coast through this class without much engagement.

Then the class trio began with Janet. She shared her story of character perseverance over emotional rent of family fabric, premature loss of innocence, and the coldness of first independence.

Second was Bob. It wasn't long before he was throwing verbal grenades in his kitchen experience, creating abstract images: natural gas explosions both in-your-face and out of sorry bowels, an accidental yet stable inverted posture, a post-death experience, and a face with anti-makeup. To my surprise, the class reinforced some of these unnatural phenomena.

And last, I experienced the undulating verbiage of Max. Wave upon wave of adjectives drowned his pathetic subject, a man of subhuman nature. Yet, I identified. No, this can't be. And Max continued relentlessly opening my wounds with this suffering creature: it couldn't speak, it would look in from the outside, pine for its beautiful obsession, and observe the lovely people in their happy erotic state. It hurt.

It is. It's me. Fourth grade, I fell for a cute brunette. But she was the smartest girl in school, and I was the dumbest boy, a poor reader. I had an inferiority complex. Then in junior high, she went on the class oversea trip. I sat in history class with the lights out, watching the trip slides. There she was on the screen, drying dishes in the galley. It hurt.

Then, in high school, I fell in love with a pompom queen, a cute brunette, popular, and I, a wallflower. I sat on the gymnasium bleachers watching her on the floor during assembly. A tilt of her hip and a spear went through my heart. I nearly fell from the bleachers. She'd giggle and laugh with her boyfriend on the school plaza at lunch time. I sat beside her in typing class and couldn't speak a word. Her father was a sports broadcaster on a local TV channel. He had his family on TV at Christmas. There she was, wishing people a merry Christmas. Again, it hurt.

Then at twenty-one, I had my first date and first kiss. What a kiss! Yes, she was a cute brunette. Yes, I was in love. But she was an experienced woman, and I was still an introvert. Then she went to work at a bank. They made a commercial. Yes, she was on TV, smiling. Yes, it hurt.

And later, the fourth-grade girl became a pediatrician at a local hospital. The hospital made a commercial, and though she didn't look like the fourth-grade girl, still it hurt.

Thrice impaled, haunted by the TV, and now Max exhumes me. And looming, the letters with poems I mailed to two celebrities, brunettes. Is the unexpected typically ugly?

The class ended. Nearly bled-out, I complimented Max on his *fine* work and exited. *I'm out. I'm safe. I can go home.*

But no, I left the class mind-bent by emotional rent, concussion, and self-exposure. With post-traumatic stress, I drove, waiting for the mental dents to pop out. I was next to the curb when a gauntlet of evergreens, like curled pythons in green camouflage, reached for me, thick, limbs licking. In turn, each sprang over the wall and low to the ground.

Shaken, I pulled in at Dunkin' Donuts. "Coffee. Coffee."

A QUESTION IN THE DARK

BY KEVIN GETCHELL

It was early in the morning before the break of day. I was out for a morning walk with that mongrel Murphy. When he was about six months old, he was found by a dog rescue organization wandering along a "rez" road on his way to Interstate 25, padding inexorably toward doom. We adopted him because he resembled the big brown dog we had recently lost to cancer. That was Buster...sweet Buster. We brought Murphy home. He was not quite as sweet.

He immediately jumped over our four foot fence, so I built a six foot fence for $1200, making him now an expensive rescue. The six foot fence cut off the view of the Jemez Mountains, making us feel like we were living in a compound; so I cut the fence down to five feet, restoring part of the view. It worked for a while; then, coyotes called in the dark. He blasted out the doggie door and over the five foot fence. Off he went to search for the erstwhile friends of his youth, tricksters in Indian myth that can enrich or challenge. We felt the challenge.

It was the darkest hour when he went over the back fence, like the Crosby, Stills and Nash song: "They say the darkest hour is just, just before the dawn, but it seems to be a long time before the dawn." Was Murphy surrounded by cunning coyotes, playfully enticing him into thinking he was one of them, only to feast on him when they brought him down? We hopelessly went to the front door. Across the street in the park, there he stood, wagging his tail.

I nailed pickets along the top of the fence, restoring it to about five foot three quarters. It worked about a week. The coyotes called again the same hour of night. Claw marks were on the slats. Murphy had clambered up the fence like a ladder. He got into a neighbor's yard. The neighbor told us that if we could not control him, he would kill him. Was this the way the new dog would be from now on? When we adopted him, the agency told us that if we *ever* thought of giving him up, we should call them. We emailed them about our plight and asked if they would take him back. Fat chance! It was clear that the organization was not going to take him back. I invested another $160 in fence slats to restore the six foot height. Murphy tried to make it over and finally failed, but I looked at my credit card balance and cursed.

Weeks later here I was walking Murphy in darkness, questioning how to get rid of him. On the west were packed neighborhoods of Rio Rancho. On the east was the unique community of Corrales which maintained its rural feel. Suddenly in that darkness before dawn, amid the clicks of Murphy's claws on the asphalt path, a startling question rang out: "Who?"

The question repeated. "Who? Who?" Relieved, I recognized the famous sentinel of the ages, an owl. As we walked in the darkness, the questioner moved from tree to tree about a hundred yards at a time, beckoning, ever asking the same question like some mediaeval wizard. I got caught up in reverie, and found myself in a quest to find the answer to what now seemed to be a transcendental question: "Who?" Murphy stopped, breaking the spell, and I stopped to pick up his excretions with the inevitable plastic bag. So much for transcendentalism.

We plodded on, me in a more realistic frame of mind, but weary because Murphy began to pull like a sled dog. Then something changed in Murphy's attitude. He started to walk less hurriedly. He savored the smell of sage. He began to behave more like sweet Buster, and I almost wept at the thought of the previous love of that precious dog. Maybe there was hope for Murphy to become less exuberant.

Again I heard the question above me on a telephone line, and staring down at me was that Great Horned Owl with dawn light outlining his huge form. He moved his head in that characteristic circular motion of owls and then belted out the question again. "Who! Who!" The meaning of the inquiry became apparent. It was a challenge to me.

The owl continued to demand. "Who? Who?" but it was as if to say: "Who will keep this needy animal? Who else would take this hapless feral dog into his home? Who will want this dog and give him a new real chance in life? Who? Who?" I found the answer within myself, "No one else but You...You."

GINGER MACGREGOR

BY MOLLY MCGINNIS HOUSTON

Ginger hobbled onto Central High School's main campus from the parking lot, auburn pony tail swinging. Even though it was early morning, she perspired from the effort under the bright August sun. Kids were milling around, standing in companionable groups, or checking their cell phones. She glanced around, not knowing any of them of course, and checked her watch. She tried to hasten her pace.

Heading for the main office building she passed a small cluster of girls, two of them bickering. As the argument rapidly escalated, it was clear the shorter of the two had the advantage. Afraid they would come to blows, Ginger stepped between them.

"Stop it," she said, trying for some show of authority.

"What's it to *you*?" The aggressive girl stepped around Ginger.

Ginger opened her mouth to utter a retort, but was stopped by a loud commanding male voice. Wincing, she turned to see a man who had to be Dr. Hart approaching them.

His navy suit, light blue shirt, and red tie portrayed a politician, more than a principal. Ignoring the other girls, but giving Ginger a quick once-over, he pointed to her and indicated with a motion of his finger that she was to come with him.

Dr. Hart opened one of the large double doors to the administrative office for her. Following behind her as they walked through the short entranceway into the lobby, his eyes took in her awkward steps. She was dressed well, wearing expensive-looking jeans and top, with a leather backpack slung over her shoulder.

Wearing a quizzical expression, he led Ginger through the noisy big office full of students clutching apparently erroneous schedule cards. They were each trying to approach one of the various secretaries' desks. Ushering her into his private office, he waved her toward a grey metal chair with a ripped fake leather seat next to the wall. A couple of nicer chairs faced his desk.

He settled his large frame into the well-padded swivel chair behind his desk. Piercing blue eyes fixed on her over his bulbous acne-scarred nose. He twisted one end of his brown handle-bar mustache between two fingers. Every few seconds his mouth twitched, from humor or irritation, Ginger couldn't tell. This unsettled her a bit, but she struggled not to show it.

She glanced at the old-fashioned school clock hanging on the wall behind him, its electric cord dangling listlessly down to an outlet. Seven fifteen. Her stomach lurched.

Finally Dr. Hart said "You must be new here since I don't remember seeing you before. And already you're antagonizing the other students."

Ginger quickly inhaled, preparing to answer his accusation.

Holding his palm up to stop her he went on, leaving her with mouth agape. "Here at Central High School, we strive for student harmony." he said. "Education is our foremost goal, and that is best achieved when our students are happy and cooperative. Unrest is always counterproductive. How long have you known Alicia?"

"Alicia?"

"The girl you were arguing with."

"Oh. Well, I wasn't exactly arguing with her. I don't even know her." Ginger was beginning to feel as exasperated as he sounded.

"By the way, young lady, what's your name?"

"Ginger MacGregor." She searched Dr. Hart's face for a hint of recognition, but none broke through his stern expression.

"At any rate," he said, "we do not like to see our older students at odds with each other. It leads to uncomfortable confrontations and sets a bad example for the younger students."

"Dr. Hart, I'm really sorry for the misunderstanding with... Alicia. But I can't possibly be late on the first day of class."

"Certainly," said Dr. Hart as he suddenly rose to his full six feet. He shooed her toward the door.

"Sorry about the way I'm dressed today. I turned my ankle last night and..." Ginger indicated a white athletic shoe before limping out.

He gawked after her as she wove her way through the mob and out the south door toward the "A" classroom building.

Ginger limped down the long hall to her first period classroom. Luckily, the back door to A-115 was open. Elbowing her way through the noisy kids to the front of the room, she set her backpack on the teacher's desk.

She quickly wrote on the chalkboard in large yellow capital letters: MS MAC GREGOR ALGEBRA ONE. A few students were watching and started shushing the others.

"Hey, I thought you wuz a student," a deep coarse voice penetrated the surprised laughter as the students slid into the closest desks.

"Good grief," Ginger said under her breath.

The seven-thirty bell rang loudly and with great authority.

I'M BUILDING A WALL

BY DAN WETMORE

I'm building a wall.

Leastways in my head. I sit up nights, memorizing the patterns of light made by new windows, new corners; a host of sounds to catalog and recalibrate for - an icemaker's infrequent avalanches, the hot water heater's indigestions, the shifts of a front door finding its evening comfort.

The cat seems to applaud my efforts with its purring, encouraging the industry. Either that or just happy for company which discerns the homage due nocturnal hours. Its sound comes in fits. I suggest her carburetor might need adjustment for altitude, like the ancient Rambler's, which so valiantly motored across Oklahoma and Texas in un-air-conditioned July. Uncle Sam has spoken, and we're once more transient, having been deemed up to the challenge of again re-potting necessarily shallow roots, this time in a desert.

I sit up late because nights are cool and expansive. Days call that illusion, revealing a dense archipelago of boxes filling the divide from porch to patio, the former trappings of 2,800 square feet needing to be squeezed into the available 1,600.

Gazing over that trackless sea is disorienting. The sameness of texture and color of a life shrouded in cardboard gifts a Zen-like emptiness, but steals the calm which comes of knowing where Figure ends and Ground begins.

Adding to the effect, the rooms are too few for the functions required, the walls too far apart in a floor plan as open as the countryside. Here are horizons prized wide by a sky more substantial than its frame. Clouds, it seems, flock to this region for post-doctoral work, having found canvas sufficient for their full genius. Here is a looming, agoraphobia-tempting openness which puts one in need of containment as insurance against insignificance.

Unsurprising then, that in the conversion of mud & clay into adobe & tile, the DNA of the land is wicked up into the houses, that the formed mirrors the expansiveness.

In new backyard, hummingbirds congregate near a butterfly bush, burbling like large ball bearings lightly rubbed together. They careen around the patio on mad paths. My oldest says it's a good argument against drinking and driving. Hopped up on nectar as they are, his discernment at twelve is spot-on. I don't divulge that my own movements feel as manic and un-channeled.

So I'm building a wall... partition to carve a sense from undifferentiated space, in hopes of securing the Goldilocks grail of "just right" teetering on the sharp crest dividing the chasms of overwhelmsion and insufficiency.

With two great rooms as palette, we envision four. One will be segregated by furniture into living room and study for my wife, the other split by a "T" wall of boxes into a spare bedroom and study for me.

And as a house holds same number of spaces (positive and negative) as it does occupants (dynamic and dormant), too few rooms includes too little storage. So that which creates usable room for people will serve double duty closeting possessions.

So I'm crafting a cairn, forming up bricks from a mixture of books, plaques, shirts, albums, trophies and tools. Dry - setting old dreams as foundation for new.

Happily that incidental's proving instrumental as well. Preoccupation with past days, it seems, has led to these. Here - albeit an oasis - is my Elba. Recent designation as a terminal Major has made the time allowed in uniform untimely iterated. The double entendre carries its full barb; connotation of "apex" having been absorbed in the womb by its twin, "demise".

Yet it serves as spur, to refute the prophecy of the powers that be, not prove so parametered as predicted. Now bereft any future's push and pull of carrot or stick, motive force is wholly internal, any remaining credit or blame irrefutably mine.

So I'm building a wall, to knock one down. To bury past incarnations and fertilize this last. Their irregular shapes lack aerodynamics, creating drag and wild perturbations in the slipstream of again early days' rapid flow. The momentum of these moments wants preserving, the vehicle for out of and into, both of which are necessary though neither necessarily desired. Because running from isn't synonymous with running to - more often its antithesis.

Most simply, I'm building - beginning's embodiment.

My drive to work takes me south on Wyoming, which parallels a rift valley the Rio Grande calls bed. October has arrived and balloons rise from the verdant lows like a curtain being raised, lilting up as bubbles in champagne, and I - in days equally buoyant and heady - seek same ascent.

I'm building a wall. Because without a wall, no door can be dug, no portal gleaned, and absent that, no distance demonstrated, no passage proven.

LIFE'S BLUEPRINT

BY AVI SHAMA

Grandmother came to visit our family soon after our arrival from Iraq to our small tent in the transition camp amid tall grasses in the middle of nowhere. She and her family had arrived to the same crowded camp a year earlier. She came to see our family and especially my mother, Nana—her older daughter, whom she had not seen since leaving Iraq.

When I saw her peeking into our tent - not sure she had the right tent, she looked the same as I had remembered her but different too. She was still wearing a white kerchief on her head, and a loving Mona Lisa smile on her face. But she had lost most of her teeth and a chunk of her weight. I suppose we all had changed in the past year; still I was startled to see her like this.

Her visit had to start with small talk as it was our custom, and it did, then move on to talking about the difficulties leaving Iraq without our assets, my long hospitalization, the unbearable, penniless and unemployed life in the transition camp, and so on. Before leaving Iraq, Nana and grandmother saw each other daily. Living only a few blocks from each other, the lives of our family— all eleven of us—and grandmother's were deeply intertwined. But the two have not seen or talked to each other for more than a year, a year of turmoil and drastic changes. So they had much to talk about, to share their experiences and store them into the memory of the extended family. This was not a visit requiring the mandatory serving of one cup of tea. Oh, no. This one was of countless cups of dark, hot tea and, for my grandmother, many cigarettes, until mother and daughter felt one again.

Grandmother loved life and she truly loved people. She was a non-stop tea drinker and a chain smoker. I don't remember ever seeing her without her tea *finjan* or a cigarette in her hand, or both. She was politically and socially aware and followed the news more than anyone else I knew. And she was an utter optimist, always seeing reality as it should be, not as it was. While we all lived in refugee tents and huts with barely anything to eat, she saw castles with vibrant gardens and happy people dining in their backyards.

I loved visiting my grandmother and spending time with her in her tent. I had been recuperating from a long illness then, and my grandmother helped my mother give me some extra attention. She became my constant motivator and cheerleader; she could even cheer up the dead in their graves.

Together, we drank hot, sweet tea and sweated in her burning tent and worked in her sweltering garden, tending to the tomatoes and the black-eyed peas. There in the garden, she would tell me about the great future awaiting me: "You would fly your own plane and land it right in front of your house. You would go to university and be able to do anything you want. The future is yours," she would conclude and look around her with a sweet smile to affirm what she had just said. I was yet to have a clear idea of what life was all about, and she already had me owning a plane and flying from one place to another as I desire.

I felt good hearing all this over and over and I would visit her tent again and again to hear her say the same exact thing again and yet again, using the same words and tone of voice. This ritual was like a mantra: it always started with drinking hot, sweet tea, moved to working in the garden, and proceeded to my owning a plane, landing it in front of my house, going to university, the future is yours, and ended with her sweet affirming smile.

This mantra never failed to transport me, however briefly, to the land of the possible, the future that can be molded. I wanted to believe her, and, in some strange way, I did. In my life of abject poverty in the transit camp, mantra-induced wishful thinking was a better reality than reality itself. For a moment, it made the hopeless—hopeful, the impossible—possible, and the unthinkable—thinkable.

At the tender age of seven, I was too young to fully comprehend what she was talking about, but felt that if I owned a plane, I surely would also have enough to eat, a good bed to sleep on, running water to wash with, and clean clothes to wear. Over time, I began to understand that the plane was a metaphor for having the means to own my life. And that made me feel good and boosted my confidence. Always. All the many times she repeated this sweet story, and the many times I could repeat it word for word the way a child can repeat childhood stories ingrained in his brain from hearing his parent read it to him over and over again.

This storytelling and motivation by my grandmother continued for a few more summers and for many tomatoes and black-eyed peas in her garden. By then her stories had been seared into my brain and formed a vague but navigable road map.

Now when I think of her, I can't help it but feel that she had given me my life's blueprint. Perhaps she knew then what I surely know now.

ROSARIO'S TEARS

BY AMARA CUDNEY

Rosario kissed her babies goodbye and promised them she'd return. The fishermen in the village said that when she left, the sea stormed and swelled, and waves crashed against the sea wall.

Rosario slipped the wad of money into the *coyote's* hand and boarded the plane to Hawaii. It was the only way she knew to feed her children.

She was unable to speak and unable to cry. The other passengers squirmed in their seats, uncomfortable with the way she stared blankly into nowhere. "Mommy? What's wrong with that lady?"

"Shhh. It's not nice to stare."

Rosario's cousin picked her up at the airport. "Come on, Cuz, time to party, let's go!"

"No, I have to work tomorrow, take me home."

The next day Patricio, her boss, picked her up. "I've got you scheduled for four condos today, okay?"

"Okay." Her eyes filled with tears. ¿Cuantos dias, cuantos? How many days before I can return? Will I ever return?

"I'll be back to check on you. Here are the keys."

"Okay."

As his van drove away, she picked up the mop bucket and cleaning supplies he'd given her. She followed the signs to number 38.

It was on the second floor, with a view of the ocean. *Is the ocean really so big?* She wondered how far away her children were as she dipped the mop into the bucket, a few tears fell into the soapy water.

She had already finished 3 residences when Patricio finally came back. He'd brought her a burrito. She barely ate. "Well, you only have one more to do. I'll be back in a couple of hours. Wait for me, okay?"

The last condo was much like the first three. Her tears never stopped and were soon soaked into the cracks in the tile floor.

A few days later, Patricio sent word to Rosario.

There wouldn't be any more work.

Mrs. Campbell returned to her home, number 38, and as she cooked dinner, she became so sad that she drank herself into a stupor and was passed out when her husband got home.

Jane Greer, in number 45, started thinking about her old boyfriend and called him, begging him to take her back. He hung up on her after telling her that he was married and to leave him alone.

Mr. Duke lay on his couch and thought about his dead wife, and sobbed the whole night.

In the light of day, the neighbors would pass each other as they walked to the beach or the golf course. "Hello. How are you?" And they saw the sadness in each other's eyes that had spilled into their lives.

They began to complain. There was something wrong with that cleaning person. Patricio couldn't keep her.

Rosario lay in her bed that night as her tears rolled down her cheeks. She knew that perhaps she'd lied to her children. Maybe she never would see her precious babies again. Her money and hope were gone. As her tears fell, they trickled to the floor and soon there was a puddle. The puddle became a flood.

Her spirit floated home to her babies and the fishermen said the clouds had broken that night with a fierce rain whose waters washed down the cobblestone streets and seeped into Rosario's mother's home.

The next morning, her cousin went to check on her. "Rosario?" The door opened and water gushed from the house. "What the....?"

Rosario lay sprawled on her bed, drowned in her own tears, holding the red ribbon her daughter had put in her hand the day she left her home in Mexico.

TWELVE DAYS IN APRIL

BY LANEY PAYNE

I was less than a month into my new job when word got around. People were reluctant to say anything. I was grateful. What would I tell them anyway? How could I put into words something there were no words for? Smiles were kind, gestures polite, but for the majority, it seemed business as usual. For our family, there was nothing usual about the minutes ticking by.

Sooner than I had expected, someone approached my desk as I was getting ready to head home. A stocky man, with a cowboy hat and pleated jeans, stood in front of my desk during the quiet hours of the late afternoon and said, "I'm sorry for your loss." *Words of sympathy,* I thought, *expressed by well-meaning people, when nothing else could be said.* "But I'd like to share something with you."

I was grateful he didn't say, "I know exactly how you feel," because, how can we? Loss is such an individual process. Instead, he said, "My wife and I lost two of our three children due to...."

That captured my attention.

* * * * *

My husband and I were privileged to be present for the birth of four grandchildren. We knew this baby was a girl; she even had a nickname - Ginger, short for Virginia, her paternal great-grandmother's namesake. Our daughter and son-in-law were pros, and by now, we knew the drill too. When the evening proved lengthy, we were told we could go home and wait for a call, which we did. Sometime after midnight we got a call to return to the hospital. It was a fifteen-minute drive. Shortly after we arrived, Virginia was born.

When the nurse held her, she let out a strong, healthy cry. She was laid in the transparent hospital bassinet. The nurse checked her vitals, and after a few minutes she was whisked away. Nothing seemed out of place. The hour was early. Adrenaline—theirs and ours—took the place of caffeine, and we knew there were tests they performed on newborns. It wasn't until our daughter said, "I want to hold my baby. How come they haven't given her to me yet?" that we took note of her lengthy absence.

We left the room to inquire. It was quiet minus our steps toward the nursery. We stood at the window. Blinds closed. A seam between the white blind and the window casing provided just enough view into a dim room, where we witnessed three people standing next to an infant. One person rhythmically squeezed their fingers in and out against a blue, bulbous, handheld ventilator pressed against a baby's face.

Medical personnel approached us and said an ambulance was en route from UNM Children's Hospital. Virginia had aspirated meconium (her first stool) deep into her lungs when she took her first cry. She was unable to breath on her own.

The next twelve days were arduous.

Our son-in-law kept a daily journal, something to share with Virginia when she was older. It detailed their daily discussions with her doctors, progress reports, setbacks, and information about the equipment used to sustain her. Every day brought new developments: some good, some bad, but we remained encouraged by the positives. Our daughter continued to pump breast milk, so when Virginia was taken off life support she would have the natural nourishment she needed.

One week, that was the initial goal. Every day past the first seven days increased her chance of survival. But on day eleven they detected a brain bleed, and that evening when they operated to alleviate the pressure, it proved too much.

As parents and grandparents, our grief was two-fold. Not that it was greater, it couldn't be. We had never lost a child. We didn't know or understand how that might feel. We all grappled with the sorrow of what would never be. But our grief held an extra component, that of watching our children and grandchildren suffer as they came to terms with the unexpected.

Yes, loss is an individual experience. But there was nothing individual about the people who surrounded Virginia. There was nothing individual about the support extended to our family. For those twelve days in April, people had collectively, if not knowingly, put themselves in our family's place, some recalling their own loss—not on a selfish level but on a conscious one—to help us deal with ours.

As for the gentleman in the cowboy hat? Well, he and his wife lost two of their three daughters. And even though each loss is separate, what they did know is that all any of us can do is to start each day, and begin again.

THE FIRST LINE

BY ROGER FLOYD

There it was, right there on the computer screen, the first line of my novel. I had just typed it. *"The small spherical probe moved silently in orbit around Mars, its cameras and sensors intently observing and recording large areas of the red planet."* Hey, not bad. I'd written a title for the novel, too, *A Visit To A Small Blue Planet*, but I changed it a few years later when I learned that book titles should be short and sweet. To grab a potential reader's interest right away. So they say.

Still, there it sat, that first line, staring back at me in a light bluish-gray font on a deep blue background. Back then I used a writing program called PC-Write on an old 80386-type computer. Ancient by today's standards, it served me well. That was even before Pentium. (Remember Pentium?) PC-Write was a type of software called shareware. That was software which you sent for by regular mail and got a free computer program on a 5¼-inch floppy disk. And, as the name said, you could share it with others.

If you liked the program you made a donation to the person who developed it. I don't remember how much I sent the company that distributed PC-Write, but I really liked it. I can still visualize that old computer and the words I wrote, now eighteen years later.

That's right, I started writing my first novel in 1998. How time has flown.

The circumstances that led up to writing that first sentence have become an indelible part of me. I lived in Cincinnati at the time, and the autumns there were spectacular, with the sugar maples and the oak trees and the sweetgums turning brilliant shades of reds, yellows, and golds. Every fall the leaves accumulated all over my yard and I had to get out and rake them up, usually in October after most of the leaves had dropped. But one clear autumn day as I raked leaves I wondered, what would a visitor from another planet think if he (she?) were to land while the leaves were falling. If no one were around to explain things to him/her, he might see the falling leaves as natural, but I think it more likely he/she'd assume the trees were dying. "Surely," the visitor would say, "living organisms don't shed essential parts of their physical being."

And therein lay the nugget of a science-fiction story.

I kept that little nugget in my head for many years, and on one fateful day in August, 1998, as I sat in the living room of my house, a sentence formed in my head. And a second, and several more. They tugged at me to write them down. Yes! Get them down! And not on paper—no, not on paper, but on the computer. It would be so much easier to write a novel on a computer than by hand or on a typewriter. I have this perfectly good writing program—let's use it. Instead of using it to write up my résumé and send out job applications, let's write a novel. This could be fantastic.

I went upstairs to the little study I'd made out of one of the four bedrooms in our house, and began to type, er, write. I wrote that one sentence and everything began to flow. Two, three, four sentences and more. A chapter appeared. I'd started a novel.

Now that I look back on it and on the rest of the first chapter I wrote that day (and subsequently revised many times over the next several years) I feel I'd done a reasonably good job. Too many "-ly" and "-ing" words, though, and probably too many "to be" words, so it would never pass muster nowadays because in the past eighteen years I've learned so much about writing.

That sentence, as well as the first several chapters, have been eliminated from the manuscript as it stands today, but it was a start, and I became a *writer*. I finished the novel and two more to complete a trilogy, and several short stories and a few poems.

And I haven't stopped yet.

SAGE CHALLENGE:

Poetry

The SouthWest Writers Association is home to many award-winning poets who share their work, insights, and talents with the rest of us. Although our talented poets send their missives throughout the year, April is *National Poetry Month*, and in that time period the *Sage* is graced with a plethora of poetic styles.

Top of the Mountain   Photo by Rose Marie Kern

STEEL TOWN GIRL

BY DR. IRENE BLEA

Freeway openings to the mill
sirens, whistles, foul smells in the air
my father making steel
mother baking bread
brothers playing in the alley
sisters out of sight
steel workers work
wives labor in small houses
me on a one way, dead end, street.

PURPLE

BY JAY BROOKS

Purple was my aunt's favorite color.
  Purple speaks of dark mystery.
Purple lingers on my eye like a sunset
  Or an old bruise, long healed.
Purple tells its own story.
  Purple Glory should be a flower.
Purple was my aunt's shroud.
  Purple starts my tears.

STAR ON THE HUNTER'S SHOULDER

BY JEANNE SHANNON

Last night we gazed at Orion.

An astronomer told us
that Betelgeuse may burst
into a supernova
tonight
next week
a thousand years from now.

Or that already
it may have done so.

And who can tell
when the light
will reach us?

GRAY

BY DENNIS KASTENDIEK

gray is the wallpaper in that dying man's bedroom
the slated air smells of gray must and darker ache
fine split ends spark at the edges of his shaggy mane
and four hundred gray taxis wait to carry him away

LIGHT TRANSITION

BY MARY E DORSEY

Daylight...
Golden firelight
ablaze across azure blue.
Fiery chariot
races to distant
horizon.

Twilight...
Royal purple ashes
spread softly in the east.
Pink embers
dance briefly in the
west.

Fading...
Faded...
Gone...

SEA AGAINST THE SHORE

BY M. A. MCDONALD

THERE'S A MILLION GRAINS OF SAND
on this great white beach
that ocean's always out there
pounding at our feet
flowing through these veins
and coursing through our hearts
that oceans always out there
tearing us apart
there's salt here in these oceans

      and salt here in my tears
      there's salt down at the mines
      it's been that way for years
      it's a rumor that we'll hear forevermore
      the crashing of the sea against the shore

YOU CAN'T BE AFRAID OF THE WATER
livin' on the beach
you can't fight the whole damn ocean
shifting at your feet
take that one thin line
that runs out from the shore
but even in the ocean's heart
you'll still hear the roar

there's salt here in these oceans
and salt here in my tears
there's salt down at the mines
it's been that way for years
it's a rumor that we'll hear forevermore
the crashing of the sea against the shore
it's a rumor that we'll hear forevermore
the crashing of the sea against the shore...

THE NEW OZYMANDIAS

BY CONNIE MORGAN

(apologies to Mr. Shelley)

I met a tourist in a nearby land
Who said, "These vile and glitt'ring towers of glass
Stand in the desert; yet, near, on the sand
Half-drunk, the shattered ones, desperately pass
Bellagio, Circus, Caesar's, and Grand
They show their planners well those passions read
Which yet survive, the gambling, wanton sots
Who test the one-armed thief, the bet, the spread

And on the inbound sign, boldy, it states
'Here lies Las Vegas', home of sin and slots
Of pricey shows, magic, and one-night dates
Four-star dinners, the strip, Mandalay Bay
Where all your fortune deteriorates
and the sandy highways stretch far away

BIRDS ON A WIRE

BY JOANNE BODIN

lined up like black clothespins
they sit sentinel-like
　waiting....
while great storm clouds form in the West
and diagonal lines of black punctuate the horizon
but the crows seem uninterested, knowing what they must do

how many times have they been on wires
lined up above city lights
　watching...
while people scurry home before the storm
before the winds siren through
open cracks in windows and howl wails of impending doom

the wire sways in the gale but the crows hold fast until
one black figure spreads its wings to signal the others

black dots of disarray lift from the
wire, take flight on a gust of wind,
scatter then congeal as if in
magical formation...

then triangulate toward the East
wind on their back, easing their journey
  into calm...

Birds on a Wire   Photo by Rose Marie Kern

SAGE CHALLENGE:

....CHEAPER THAN THERAPY

We asked our members how they handled the stress in their lives. What options do they employ rather than paying for expensive therapy? The next two stories show how these authors use their passions to mitigate the frustrations in their life.

HARPING: CHEAPER THAN THERAPY

BY MICHELLE BUCHANAN

The letter arrived on the last day of July. "This is to inform you that due to budgetary issues, your position of Homebound Teacher will no longer be assigned an Educational Assistant. If you require such assistance submit a written requisition for personnel to meet you at the Homebound address."

I choked out the words, "I can't do the job like this! Requisition someone like a sack of potatoes? What about liability?"

Seeing the pain on my face, my husband said, "Just go retire. You have the years."

His words zipped across my forehead like Santa spilling toys. Without a second thought I drove to the APS office that Friday, at 3:45pm.

"Hi, I need to retire today," I calmly said to the lady, who sat alone waiting for her week to end. The new school session would start Aug. 1st. and I had no time to interview for a different position. They must have planned it that way.

"Are you going to take a helicopter?" she asked

"What?"

"I need your birth certificate, these forms filled out, and a letter to the superintendent, by 5 pm."

I raced to my bank across town, retrieved the certificate from the safe deposit box and arrived back at her feet with ten minutes to spare.

She clucked her tongue. "I don't know, I need special permission to send a fax to Santa Fe. It costs two dollars.

She took the bills and I got retired. With children still in school and wondering what I had just done, I went home.

I'm retired!" I said as I opened the door.

"What do you want to do now?" asked my wonderful husband.

"I'd like to play the harp!"

He smiled, not the least bit perturbed, and said, "I have a brochure for kits. I can build one for you, but I think you should sew up your fabric. It's a fire hazard."

You may think this thought about playing a harp occurred in some previous discussion, or that I was a trained musician, or that I'm just making this up. The words exploded out of the blue and into my new reality as a retired teacher.

My confident husband found the catalogue, we looked at pictures, and wondered which kit we should order. I knew we couldn't afford to buy one already made.

We selected the largest harp, because I'm tall, not even thinking whether it could fit in a car. The kit came, and my Renaissance Man let the wooden pieces acclimate to our dry climate for at least a month before he even began construction. By the new year I had a thirty-six string Celtic harp, in cherry. There was a book, "Teach Yourself the Celtic Harp," and lessons on-line, plus a welcoming harp community here in town.

The fabric stash turned into a costume business, and soon I was harping at festivals, Renfaires, and retirement homes. My harp took me to playing hospice as well as weddings, funerals and house parties. Wherever I went, people would ask, "Where do harps come from?" This resulted in extensive research, and my first novel, "Scota's Harp."

To say that harping is cheaper than therapy is a massive understatement. Having beautiful sound penetrate my chest as I hold the harp close is a feeling surpassed only by the smiles and blessings I receive from playing. Tearful thanks from a grieving relative or seeing a child's joyous face when I let them take a strum have replaced the tragedies of my Special Ed students' lives.

SWIMMING: CHEAPER THAN THERAPY

BY ANNETTE THEIS

Two things happened the day my dad died. I said my last good
-bye to Dad. And I went swimming.

My dad would have wanted me to go swim.   He knew how
much I loved to swim and always laughed when I said, "swimming
is my Prozac." I left the hospital and headed to the pool hoping the
emptiness I felt would abate by the time I finished my workout.

While I swam my first few laps I remembered the first time
Dad took me to the pool. It was a warm summer afternoon but the
water was cool. He picked me up and walked slowly into the water
so he could gauge my reaction to the temperature. When I didn't
flinch, he started swishing me back and forth in the water. A small
wave formed with each swish then I would bump into that wave
when he swished me the opposite direction.

That day I realized how much I liked being in the water. Rather
than being scared I felt weightless and free. More importantly I felt
protected and comforted in the water.

Somewhere around lap 10 I suppressed a giggle as I recalled
how he picked me up high over his head then dropped me in the
water. I wasn't afraid because as soon as I fell into the water he'd

scoop me up and ask if I wanted to do it again. My laughter said it all.

Around lap 14 I began to sob (yes you can cry in the water) when I flashed on my Dad's young cancer-free face with pool water dripping from his dark curly hair into his laughing eyes. I sobbed because I'd lost my hero, the Dad who taught me to love and trust the water.

Finally, by lap 20 a calm settled in and I focused on my breath, counted my strokes and started to relax. A rhythm consumed me and 40 lengths later I left the pool feeling stronger and more equipped to deal with the rest of the day.

Swimming is therapy. It never fails to center me on the worst of days and when the day is going well it's just icing on the cake. I've made swimming part of my daily routine-like eating and sleeping so I don't have to wonder if I'll swim

I just get up and head to the pool.

I've had friends say I'm addicted to swimming. But it's better for me than drugs or alcohol. I crave the calm I feel after swimming. It takes the edge off too many cups of coffee and helps burn all the calories I get from eating half a carton of Bunny Tracks ice cream more often than I should.

I'm in such a good mood after I swim (while all those endorphins are rushing through my body) that I'm not as apt to yell at the crazy Albuquerque drivers I encounter on my drive home. Swimming has probably saved my life more than once–and not just by keeping me from drowning!

Swimming has introduced me to friends I wouldn't have known otherwise. It's always easier to start a conversation about swimming. I've read that social connections for people of "a certain age" are important. My conversations at the pool, because they are face to face are far better than anything I can do on the computer. And, if an acquaintance from the pool happens to become a good friend that's even better.

Current research says that blood flow to the brain during exercise helps decrease dementia and stroke. I can't think of a better reason to get in the pool since my mother had dementia.

My daily swim was the best therapy the weeks and months after my dad died. I felt comforted and protected in the water much as my Dad had comforted and protected me growing up. Swimming brings me full circle.

When I swim I am lighter, both physically and mentally and closer to meditation than I can ever be sitting quietly in a room. My thoughts become as clear as the water that surrounds me and when confronted with a dilemma before I hop in the pool I usually have the beginnings of a solution by the time I'm showering after my swim.

I can't think of a better way to alleviate stress, burn calories, meditate and solve world problems – all in my hour swim!

JULY, 2018 *SAGE* CHALLENGE:

THE RED, WHITE, AND BLUE

Holidays make good challenges for writers because they are filled with memories. But unlike the "How I Spent Summer Vacations" kids were forced to write, our members bring a great deal of life experiences to their work. The next piece by Jim Tritten, former Air Force pilot, brings a different perspective to the deeper meaning of Independence Day.

TAKING OFF THE UNIFORM

BY JIM TRITTEN

Jasmine and I entered the medicine circle, arm in arm, from the east, the direction of the rising sun and the new day. Dusty tan stones lined the sandy path to the center. The acrid tang of burning sage hung in the air. We turned to the south and walked to the makeshift altar. We poured cool water from an earthen jug over each other's hands, and the water dripped into a large yellow and red basin. We dried our hands on thin cotton towels, smiled at one another and turned around to face the center of the circle.

Our medicine man, David Singing Bear, a Marine Corps veteran of Cherokee descent, chanted while he waited for us with a Storm Cloud ceremonial blanket. He unfolded the sacred cloth, woven in red and black, grey and white, and raised it to the sky. He called on his gods to bless us as a couple, and me as a returning service member. Based on Native American rituals that welcome home warriors after battle, this ceremony was the culmination of an eight-day retreat the National Veterans Healing & Wellness Center in Angel Fire, New Mexico.

David draped the woolen Storm Cloud over our heads and shoulders. Jasmine and I, who had been married then for 20 years, spoke to each other in total privacy. I thanked her for being there for me when I needed her most, when I was at the deepest depths of PTSD. David resumed his chant and we emerged. He continued his song, and I felt lighter, as though a burden had been eased.

We walked back to the center of the circle and turned to the north, and there stood two colonels, one in Air Force blue, and one in Army green. They stood at attention, next to a sculpture of a rifle with bayonet in the ground, helmet on the stock. I adjusted my frame, stood ramrod straight, felt my heels click together, and raised my right arm. I executed a very crisp, very Navy salute. They slowly returned the salute and said, "Welcome home, Sailor."

I remember dropping my arm, and not much else. My chest shuddered, eyes shut against the sting of tears, and I lost all sensation of sound, smell, or my feet touching the ground. Jasmine took my elbow and led me back out through the center of the medicine circle, along the sandy path lined with stones. The first thing I saw through the tears, and the first thing I could feel was the rest of my fellow veterans and their spouses, my village, my community, clapping me on the back, hugging me with abandon, welcoming my return. I had taken off the uniform twenty-seven years earlier, but today I was finally home.

"Taking off the Uniform," previously appeared in *As You Were: The Military Review*, November 2016. This story won 1st place in the 2018 National Veterans Creative Arts Festival. http://militaryexperience.org/taking-off-the-uniform/

INTERACTIVE POETRY

Photo by Joanne S. Bodin

In April 2017, two renowned poets—Joanne Bodin and Jeanne Shannon—shared a form of poetry writing known as *Exquisite Corpse* during an SWW meeting. They then lead the members present in an interactive poetry writing experience. An introduction to that style and some poems created during that meeting follow in this section.

INTRODUCTION TO EXQUISITE CORPSE POETRY

BY JOANNE BODIN

Exquisite Corpse, also known as **exquisite cadaver**, is a method by which a collection of words or images is collectively assembled. Each collaborator adds to a composition in sequence, either by following a rule, as in adjective, noun, adverb etc.. or by being allowed to see only the end of what the previous person contributed.

The technique was invented by surrealists and is similar to an old parlor game called *Consequences*, in which players write in turn, on a sheet of paper, fold the paper to conceal part of the writing, then pass it to the next player for further contribution. Surrealism's principal founder, Andre Breton said the diversion started about 1925.

Later the game was adapted to drawing and collage, producing a result similar to children's books in which the pages were cut into thirds, the top third showing the head of a person or animal, the middle third the torso, and the bottom third the legs, with children having the ability to "mix and match" by turning pages.

The following Exquisite Corpse poems were written during a SouthWest Writers' meeting in celebration of National Poetry Month in April. In honor of the bards and word-weavers, mainstay of cultural preservation, we came together for an interactive experience in the poetic tradition of *exquisite corpse* Members sat at tables in small groups and after the poetry exercise was over one person from each table read the group exquisite corpse poem into a mic and the entire event was added to our You Tube videos of speakers and events.

SWW Members who collaborated on the following
Exquisite Corpse poems:

Arlene Hoyt-Schulze
Kent Langsteiner
Don DeNoon
Jay Brooks
Yvonne Williams Casaus
Gail Hamlin
Dan Wetmore
Robert Staub
Ellen Welker
Robert Spiegel
Roger Floyd
Sam Moorman
Dennis Kastendiek

EXQUISITE CORPSE #1

The man is walking a white dog on the beach.
Searching for a person, a lost time, a feeling.
Of sad fields, where children played before the war.
Mothers, fathers, sisters, brothers call out. No answer. All is lost.
Boxcars, flatcars, lights and guards, where are they?
They come home again to settle their grievances, their thirst.
Craving the justice of equality, to drink the wine of freedom.
They come in their hundreds, their thousands, only a promise to their
children left to keep.
But children know little of promises and less of night.

EXQUISITE CORPSE #2

The clock is upside down
Surreal, as if time is frozen
Like a sunset permanently captured on canvas
A moment frozen in time
A moment unforgettable and rich
A time to be relived as long as life remains.

A piece of driftwood washes onto the ocean's shore
Resembling a pony in flight
Dancing and playing amid early spring wildflowers
Barefoot and carefree, our hearts once again set free
Like the wind in the willows
The foaming dance of water among the seaside rocks

EXQUISITE CORPSE #3

the clock is upside down
Phinious Duck withheld a frown
the forty seventh from that week alone.
smiles in dirty underwear and drizzling tears
held momentarily by shaggy suspenders.
ah, love has such strange clothes
which cannot hide its soul
or turn the clock aright again
without avail, as spring into summer and
day taking flight.
the ribbons of sunrise shimmer
as the ants and the rabbits look on.

EXQUISITE CORPSE #4

An artist throws paint at an easel
It misses and oozes down the wall.
It's a two year-old's squirt gun
Lethal as an imagination's aim
Scattering with spirit, divinely guided
The soul moves gracefully to the great beyond
And returns again gracefully
A gazelle perfecting pirouettes,
Eyes sparkling and glistening with joy
The puppy waited for his treat.
And shared it with his siblings

EXQUISITE CORPSE #5

An artist throws paint at an easel.
His eyes focus on the orange spot.
The orange is the one I brought here.
 My words taste like orange spine.
 When I hear the chime of the microwave,
 then I enjoy orange with my friend,
 and blend our evening into bliss.
 Only when our bodies touch
 do we feel so happy and laughter rises like a bird.

SAGE CHALLENGE:

MYSTERY

JUST A LITTLE TOO PERFECT

BY DON TRAVIS

What time was it!

I sat up and glanced at the clock on Luann's bedside table. One fifty-five in the morning. Good Lord! I'd fallen asleep after she wore me out around midnight. What the hell would I tell my wife?

While scrambling around in the dark trying to separate my duds from Luann's, I fabricated my yarn. I'd been at a bar. The Stoop. With two of my associates. Bart. Yeah, Bart was a barfly. And Christopher was a hanger-on.

I rushed into the kitchenette for a swig of bourbon to put alcohol on my breath before racing to my Lexus parked on a nearby street. My tires burned rubber on the way home as I delicately balanced the need for speed with the need to avoid getting a ticket.

On the approach to the broad drive of my North Valley home, the perfect symmetry of the brick and stone edifice struck me anew. A perfect home. A perfect job. A perfect wife. A perfect *life*. Except something was off about it.

An auditor with a large accounting firm, I was pissed when they brought in someone from the outside to take over management when my boss retired. This perfect home suffered from aging plumbing and a structural fracture in trusses supporting a heavy clay tile roof.

Helen, the beautiful, educated, cultured woman I married, was very good in dealing with people. A perfect mate for my profession. But all that beauty hid sharp talons capable of ripping the psyche as well as the flesh.

I entered the house through the garage to find Helen in a recliner absorbed in a New Mexico family saga novel called *The Eagle's Claw* by local author Donald T. Morgan.

"Good book?" I asked catching a scent of the rosewater she usually wore.

"It holds my interest." She arched an eyebrow. "Aren't we getting home a little late? Without even a telephone call."

"Met some of the guys at the Stoop." I spun my tale of lies, submitted to the inevitable questions, and considered myself lucky. Until I turned to walk away.

"What's that caught in your belt?" Her voice hardened a little more with each deliberate word.

A chill ran down my back. With no idea what she was talking about, I stood glued to the carpet until she bounded out of the chair and snatched something that came free with a tug of my shorts. A pair of Luann's pink, delicately laced panties. Oh, Lord! So much for carefully separating my clothing from hers.

Needless to say, my life was not so perfect any longer. Banished from the house, I now lived in a motel room. News of my marital problems spread after Helen's divorce attorney interviewed Bart and Christopher about our non-existent night on the town. My problems affected my work. I'd be immersed in a client's tax problem and find myself distracted by what had been my perfect life... before Pantygate.

After my new boss gave me a veiled warning about shaping up or shipping out, I woke to the fact that I might end up with *nothing* of that life left. Any divorce court in the land would award Helen the house and half my assets—there went the perfect house and the perfect wife. With my job in jeopardy, the rest of it could vanish, as well.

Frightened, I undertook a search for salvation—financial, not spiritual. Although I could probably use some of that, as well. I didn't realize how desperate I was until I remembered Nick Shazinski.

We'd gone to school together back in the day but didn't pal around. From the wrong side of town, Nick ran with a rough crowd. The local cops knew him well, even before we graduated. But Nick and I had always gotten along in an arms-length sort of way.

I'd lost touch with him, but we reconnected one day in the office of a client named J. Butterfield Thomas, known to be the local mob's preeminent attorney. My old friend did some of the lawyer's investigative work. Nick and I went to lunch a couple of times, and I even had him over to the house, mostly to see how my socially conscious wife would react. But Nick cleaned up well, and Helen seemed drawn to his rough side

I'd heard enough stories to suspect Nick might be the solution to my problem. So I put in a call to my old buddy to let him know I had a problem.

"I heard. You wanna talk it over?"

"Yes, but in private," I said.

"My place or Butter's office?"

"Somewhere we won't be noticed. By anyone."

"Oh ho. I get your drift. It's that serious, huh?"

Uncomfortable over saying too much over the phone, I simply agreed.

An hour later, I nosed my Lexus into a big deserted warehouse on Commercial SE. Nick had chosen well. It didn't appear anyone visited the premises often. As I got out of the car, Nick walked out of what had been the office when this was a functioning business.

"Thanks for meeting me." I licked my lips and tasted fear. *Could I go through with this?*

"Problems, huh?"

"Big time. Ones that call for desperate measures." I turned away to avoid looking at him as I spoke the fateful words. "I want to hire you. I brought $5,000 as a down payment."

"Sorry, pal. But I already got a job. But thanks for the five grand bonus."

My back prickling, my heart somewhere below my belly, I turned to find him screwing something long and chilling onto the end of a wicked-looking handgun.

MYSTERY OF THE DEAD SISTERS

BY LYNN ANDREPONT

Dead of night, October 1940. Outside the rain turns to sleet. I hear it rapping on the windows of our small office. My partner and I gulp down strong, black cups of java as we try to make sense of a double-murder case gone ice cold, just like the weather.

"Let me get this straight," I say to Diane. "All we have is a single secondhand witness, someone's auntie, who hears the story from her niece, who's off her nut, about two dames, sisters, snuffed out at different but unknown times, at unknown locations, up north somewhere, and we have no motive, no evidence...and no bodies, right?"

"You got it, boss. I grilled the aunt on all the details."

Diane's a real sleuth, the best partner a private dick...make that a private jane...could ever hope to have.

"Maybe," she adds, glancing at her notes, "none of it even happened. The whole bit just a homicidal scam, a ruse, a waste of our time. Still, auntie wants reassurance her niece isn't headed for the slammer."

If you need someone to crack a case wide open, retrieve stolen goods, infiltrate the mob, pinch a couple of goons, keep some innocent kid out of the clink, then I'm your gal. At least I was. Not much ever happens out here in the dustbowl boonies these days. At least this cock-and-bull story intrigues me.

"Oh, yeah," Diane crosses over to the window. "There's a pair of shoes, reportedly belonging to the first tomato done in."

"The sister supposedly crushed to smithereens by some large falling object?" I ask.

"That's her," Diane snickers, "one splattered tomato."

"Could've been an accident."

"The niece claims the monkey men were sure it was no accident."

"Monkey men?"

"Yeah, the other sister's hatchet guys. Seems they had a vendetta for the niece...and then there's her little dog."

"What's the lowdown on the mutt?'

"Got in a scrap with some neighbor back home so was nabbed for the pen, the big house for pooches. The niece tells auntie she thinks this neighbor might be a third sister because she looks just like them."

"Could this be a motive?"

"Nah, the pup managed to bolt and return home."

I've been around the block a few times, but I've never had a case like this. You need three things in this gumshoe business to succeed: smarts, compassion, and guts. I think I have things figured out and suddenly the tables turn on me. I feel for this aunt and her niece. But perhaps my sympathy is misplaced. Maybe I got it all wrong. Could even be a lousy frame up. But I won't back off. I'll gather all that's clever, devoted, and gritty in me to get to the bottom of this.

Murder is murder.

"So when," I ask, "does the niece spill the beans on these murders?" Something doesn't add up.

"After the tornado," Diane looks at her notes again. "She tells auntie about walking for miles on some brick road to a field where she's served up lullaby juice, some poppy-pollen drug that puts her to sleep. Who knows what's real and what could just be a dream?"

"Are there other players in this escapade?" I pour myself another cup o' joe to keep my own eyes open.

"A carny guy, a midget gang, some princess doll, and a trio of clowns."

Clowns. The world is full of them.

"Auntie also mentioned the big cheese, some wise guy said to have all the answers."

"Wish I could meet that bird. I'd have a few questions for him."

"Turns out, he's just a chiseler, a con, a crumb. At least that's what the niece told her auntie."

"And the other sister, how does she bite it?"

"Acid."

"Jeeze!"

"But the niece swears she didn't know it was acid. She's a prisoner in the sister's joint, see. The monkey men have the place locked up tight. The sister wants to put the screws on those shoes the niece is wearing, the ones belonging to the other vamp and gifted to her by the princess, but they won't come off, see, unless she's iced. The niece just wants to go home and manages to escape with the help of Fido and the three clowns. But before they get away, the sister stops them, see, and torches one of the clowns. The niece grabs a nearby bucket and tosses whatever's in it to douse the fire; some splashes on the sister's puss, and so long Irene."

"Was that the sister's name?"

"Nah, boss, it's just an expression, like Fido ain't the name of the dog neither. Funny thing, though, the sister disintegrates but the clown ain't hurt at all. Must've been wearing protective rags, some kind of flame- and acid-retardant underclothes. But then, this stuff doesn't happen every day in Kansas."

"And all we've got to go on are a pair of shoes."

"Yep, ruby-red slippers."

You think you know where you stand and someone throws you behind the eight-ball. You've got nothing. You're left looking like some kind of sucker. Sure, you think you've got some Ace, some Bruno pegged for theft, kidnapping, maybe murder, but turns out you're fingering the wrong ringer—your main suspect is a little lost girly who just wants to go home.

"Diane, seems to me these sisters got what might've been coming to them, and the niece..."

"Her name is Dotty, boss."

"Well, I say Dotty was in the wrong place at the wrong time."

Oh well, the rain has stopped. Time for us to head home. There's no place like it.

Maybe I'll just leave this one for that know-it-all wizard to solve.

SAGE CHALLENGE:

TRAVEL

SWW members write in many styles and formats. Their travels inspire stories and articles which are either combined into book form or sold as articles to travel publications.

Some stories offer advice, others insight and, as in the first story, warning.

Wingtip   Photo by Rose Marie Kern

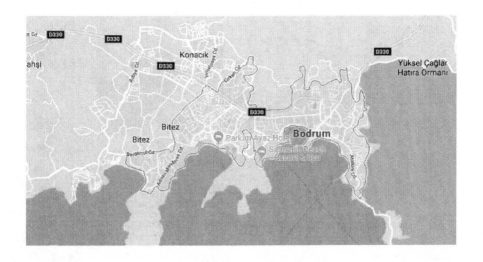

BODRUM

BY PATRICIA CONOWAY

"I'm going to love Turkey, I just know it," I said to myself. It was the summer of 1976. I'd been traveling for about a month and the world was my oyster. I took a mini bus to Bodrum, a beautiful, whitewashed town which sat nestled around a lovely bay and beach area. It looked more like Greece than Turkey and was stunning with its clear blue sky and azure water gently lapping at the shore.

I was the only foreigner and the only woman on the bus. I'd been warned about traveling alone in Turkey, especially as a blue-eyed blonde. I was wondering what all the fuss regarding Turkish men was about as most of the men I'd met were either extremely polite or helpful, or kept their distance. As I stepped off the bus, a handsome, powerfully built man in his late twenties approached me.

"Do you need accommodation?" he asked in very broken English. Since Bodrum at that time wasn't in tour books, I knew this might be the best or only way to find an inexpensive room.

"Yes, thank you." I replied.

"This way," he gestured as I followed. We walked a few blocks to an apartment building as we exchanged introductions. His name was Mustafa. On the second floor of the building was the room for rent. The apartment was occupied by a family of three: a couple and a young baby. Mustafa told me the woman was his cousin. He pointed to a small room with a dresser and bed.

"This is your room. It costs $1.00 US."

"Where's the shower?" I asked. He led me to a separate room with a hole in the floor, the Turkish version of a toilet. Adjacent to it was another small space with a shower head on the wall and a drain. I noticed with dismay there was only one faucet, indicating a cold-only option for a shower. I was sweaty, dusty and having my period. I'd been looking forward to a hot shower and an early night. I sighed, and handed him a dollar.

"Would you like to join me at a cafe for some chai?" he asked.

"That would be great!" I replied. I left my bags in the room, grabbed my fanny pack with some money and followed him to a lovely outdoor cafe. Over chai, he told me he'd been working in Austria as a guest (temporary) worker and was back in Bodrum for the summer. He asked if I'd like to have a Turkish bath that afternoon. I thought "What LUCK" to myself and asked where it was.

"Just five minutes from here," he replied. "We can go when you finish your chai."

I thought for a minute, unsure of what to do. I knew I trusted Turks in general, had no reason not to, but was he the same as the others? My desire for a hot soothing Turkish bath overcame my trepidation. After all I had no reason NOT to trust him, did I? I was staying with his relatives, wasn't I? I got into the car.

True to his word, Mustafa delivered me to the bath in five minutes. There was no one there but the woman at the door, who collected my $1.00 in Turkish money and impassively motioned me inside. I hesitated again, looking back at Mustafa.

"I will wait for you here." he smiled. "Enjoy your bath!"

I went inside, found a cubicle and undressed. I was so tired and so eager for a bath that I only gave cursory attention to the fact that I was the only person in the entire place. In the bathing area I doused myself with hot, steaming water. Slowly, luxuriously I poured shampoo into my hair and massaged my scalp. It felt heavenly. I heard a noise and looked up. Mustafa was walking towards me, naked, with an erection.

I was speechless. In that moment, I realized how truly stupid I'd been. He came over to me, pushed me back on the marble and started to climb on top of me.

"NO!" I cried, "NO!" a second time, screaming it. He put his hand over my mouth. I was so soapy his hand slipped and I tried to twist away.

"Stop, leave me alone!" I screamed again, wondering whatever had happened to the woman outside as we struggled on the soapy, wet floor. He outweighed me by at least forty pounds and was in top condition. There was a rock I managed to grab. I tried bashing it into the back of his head. He grabbed my arm and easily flung it away. He was on top of me again. My strength was weakening. I couldn't continue fighting him much longer.

I was more enraged than frightened. I wanted to kill him, hurt him, punish him but I didn't have the physical strength. He kept trying to spread my legs and I fought desperately to keep them together, slipping and sliding. In my desperation I screamed out loud: "Dear God, please help me!" My voice echoed off the walls. He put one hand over my mouth while the other held my wrists above my head as I continued to squirm.

In a flash, a lightning bolt, it came to me. Somewhere in the recesses of my brain I remembered Moslems don't touch a woman when she is "unclean."

"Wait!" I rasped, wresting my mouth from behind his hand. "Do you understand the word *menstruation*?"

"Are you sure?" he raised his head and looked into my face for the first time since he'd entered the bath. He stopped trying to spread my legs.

"I swear it!" I hissed. His erection went limp. He rolled off me.

"Go, get dressed," he said quietly.

I ran in those clumsy clogs from the steaming bath, not even pausing to rinse off the soap in my hair or on my skin. I dressed as quickly as I could.. He came to the changing cubicle and respectfully stood outside, though there was only a curtain between us.

"Are you finished?" he asked.

"No," I replied. "But there's something I want you to see." I pulled the curtain aside enough to thrust my bloody underpants in his face. He backed away in horror and stumbled out of the changing area. I waited a few minutes, then stepped outside.

The woman who'd taken my money was gone. He'd clearly paid her to leave so he could rape me. He was waiting for me at the door, his hands filled with large stones. I looked at him contemptuously.

"You take, you throw at me, please," he begged, his eyes filled with tears. "You will be like my sister."

"If I hadn't been menstruating, you would have raped me, evet (yes)?" He looked at his feet, ashamed, contrite.

"Evet." he replied in a low, small voice.

"Please just take me back. I'm not going to throw stones at you."

He politely escorted me to the car, even opening my door for me, and drove back to town in silence. Before he left, he begged me again: "Please, you will be my sister. Please allow me to take you out in a boat tomorrow. We fish, have lunch, I not hurt you." Exhausted and spent, I just shook my head.

The next morning I quietly packed and made my way to the mini bus. The whitewashed buildings gleamed in the early morning sun and the waves sparkled on the sea as the bus pulled away.

ON FOOT THROUGH THE COUNTRY OF PAINTER FRANTISEK MORIC NÁGL

BY MONIKA GHATTAS

"Kostelní Myslova", the partially rusted sign read. How would one pronounce this? It must be the name of this village we are walking through. Forty houses or so. Obviously nothing remarkable here.

A few steps further into the village Aloijz, our Czech hiking guide, motioned us to stop. He made a brief phone call and then announced unexpectedly, "A guide will give us a short talk about this village and then take us on a tour. She will be here in a minute."

I didn't read the walking schedule for today, so this was news to me. But a short stop was good. It was too early for lunch, so I pulled a baggie of almonds out of a side pocket and looked around. Nothing noteworthy about this small village, except perhaps the two-story house that stood on a small hillock behind us. Unlike all the whitewashed farmers' houses with their tidy yards and flowering fruit trees, this one was evidently deserted and in ruins. The yard overgrown with weeds, no window glass, the roof caving in on all sides.

Today was one of our longer walking days through the Czech countryside.

We toured Vranov Castle in the morning and were scheduled to spend the night in picturesque Telc. This Sierra Club trip had been advertised as "Walking from Vienna to Prague." Not literally, of course, but there were plenty of walking days through this lovely countryside of fields and forests, quaint villages, and, occasionally, the rusty, hidden remnants of a terrible war.

A young woman came from a side street and warmly greeted our guide. "Please welcome Anna. She will be our guide for a special journey through the countryside. But first she wants to say a few words."

She was in her early forties, wearing faded jeans, and a large macrame' bag on her shoulder. She smiled and began her story. "About 15 years ago I married someone from this village. I was an outsider and not really accepted by the people living here. So I spent a lot of time walking around and trying to learn as much as possible about this place. What especially intrigued me was that house over there."

She pointed towards the dilapidated house I had already noticed.

"I asked neighbors, the grocer, everybody I met about the history of that house. It seemed that nobody knew anything about the former owners or why it was in such a poor condition."

She paused a moment and then continued, "It seemed to me that people were anxious to change the subject. Perhaps they knew something, but didn't want to talk about it."

But she continued in her quest. Younger people in the village began to take an interest in her questions and she slowly knitted together the bits and pieces she learned about the former inhabitants of this house.

"It belonged to a small farmer by the name of Franticek Nágl, who lived there with his wife and two children. He was also a gifted painter who sold his watercolors at the Saturday market in Jihlava, a few kilometers from here."

She took an envelope of postcards from her bag and passed them around. Pictures of the surrounding countryside and nearby villages. "These are some of his watercolors that we had made into postcards. Please take one."

"In 1943, they came for Franticek Nágl. Who were they? The Nazis—Germans and Czech sympathizers, who took the painter and his family to Theresienstadt, where he taught drawing to some of the other inmates. Eventually, he and his family perished in Auschwitz. He was the only Jew in this small village that numbered about 150 people."

She detailed the arduous process of prying information from the reluctant villagers. It was as if a communal amnesia had erased the memory of something that happened a long time ago.

"But I persisted in my quest to restore the details of this tragic event. And gradually a few other villagers offered their help," she recounted quietly.

"We began thinking about some kind of memorial. It was difficult. We didn't have the means to restore the house. Besides, there were no artifacts that recalled the life of Franticek Nágl. But we did find many of his watercolors."

Our little group of 11 hikers waited quietly for her to continue. A sadness had touched all of us, but we were also hoping, unconsciously perhaps, for something good to emerge.

"So please follow me and let me show you what we put together."

A few hundred feet down a narrow path, she stopped. In front of us were fields of yellow rape seeds in bloom. And to the right was a pole with a postcard image of these exact fields printed from one of Nágl's watercolors. From there we walked to a pond with overhanging willow branches and a small fishing dock. Again there was the same postcard image printed from a painting finished years ago. It was attached to a pole and wrapped in a protective film together with a brief explanation. Our next stop was a forest clearing filled with dappled light. The identical postcard picture was displayed on a pole. And so we followed the painting route of Franticek Nágl for over an hour.

Eventually we reached a little hill that overlooked the valley below. Two long benches surrounded a large, rectangular table made from a rough limestone slab. A colonnade of birch trees defined that special spot.

"By the time we reached here, the whole village was engaged in our project," Anna explained. "The men hewed this limestone slab from those mountains over there and planted all of the trees you see here. We also received some help from civic associations in Telc and in Berlin."

A shiny brass plate attached to the slab marked the ceremonies that celebrated the completion of this memorial in 2002. Officials from Prague and the German ambassador joined the village and surrounding countryside to mark this special occasion.

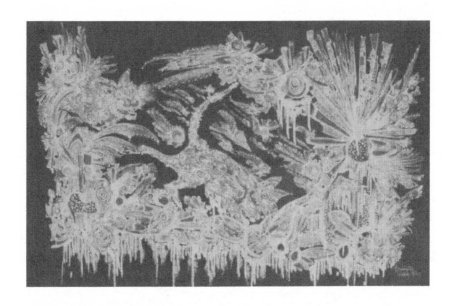

UNPACKING THE BATIK PAINTING

BY NEILL MCKEE

When I returned from Indonesia in January of 1970, my house in Kota Belud, Sabah, Malaysia smelled musty. Mold grows quickly in North Borneo when rooms are left closed and unaired, and I had been away during almost two months of school vacation. I had completed over half of my two-year assignment as a Canadian volunteer teacher at Kota Belud's secondary school.

I really missed Rebecca, my traveling companion in Indonesian. Before flying to Singapore, I had dropped in to see her at her school in Sarawak and invited her to join me in Central Java, after her classes ended. I had been somewhat surprised by her spontaneous acceptance.

I played my new Bob Dylan LPs on my little record player—"Girl from the North Country" and "Lay Lady Lay." The songs brought back my time with her. While the music played, I unpacked and sorted my belongings. I took out the only cultural memorabilia I had collected along the way, a batik cloth painting purchased in Indonesia, which I unfolded and tacked to the living room wall. It was bright yellow-orange on a black background—more shocking than I'd remembered—with the artist's name and date inscribed in the bottom righthand corner: "Bambongodoro Wokidjo 1969."

As I stared at the painting, the whirling ceiling fan caused it to shudder and come to life. Its intricate elements rippled, stirring up my experiences during the past few weeks. The four-legged beast at its center, lurched downward. Another beast's head, emerging from the upper left, had cat-like whiskers and scary eyes, but both had ears like delicate butterflies. Strange fish-like creatures with ornamental tails flew in the dark sky. Detached eyes and volcano-like formations erupted in winged patterns. Streams of a blood-like lava oozed downwards. The whole scene flowed counter-clockwise, chaos emerging into a kind of symmetry; pockets of stars pulling me inwards towards black spaces of unpacked memories.

* * * * *

Just a few weeks earlier, I had been lying on a straw mat on the deck of a freighter, gazing at the stars. I could see the Southern Cross near the horizon. European explorers of long ago, the first to venture into the southern hemisphere, discovered this constellation as guidance in navigating these waters, where they could no longer sight the North Star and Big Dipper. For me, as for them, it was a beacon in the night sky, inviting me southwards into the unknown.

BENEFIT FROM SENDING ILLUSTRATED EMAILS ON LONG TRIPS

BY CAROL KREIS

Regale your family and friends with e-mails and photos while you live it up for months on end in other parts of the world. They enrich the journey and are a plus for writers.

When my husband, Chuck, and I planned our biggest trip ever, many were curious how we would handle a five-month, around-the-world trip on our own. After all, we were getting long in the tooth. At the time my spouse was almost 80, and I was 74.

Acquaintances made remarks such as: "What? You're going to go around the world in five months? Will it be by ship? Is it some kind of a tour? I would love to see your itinerary."

I decided our travel adventures could be turned into a book with suggestions for older folks with wanderlust.

Gather e-mail addresses

Close to 100 friends gave me their e-mail addresses so I could e-mail them trip updates. I hoped that some of them might buy my book (still in progress).

Why send e-mails?

Why not post photos with comments on Facebook instead? They can be shared there, but it may be wisest to wait until after your trip has ended. I've heard warnings about not letting the world know through social media that you are away from home for an extended period of time. Besides, not all seniors use Facebook. Most of us use e-mails, though. Short quips work well on Facebook, but e-mails are better for complete thoughts.

Travel journals are another way to keep track of experiences, but illustrated e-mails have a lot of merit. They are an easy way to capture plenty of the highs and lows of travel while you are bouncing from one country to the next on a long journey.

Responses to on-the-road e-mails encourage more writings

At times it can get lonely, being away from home for many months. Every time I sent out the e-mails, I heard back from 10 to 15 people right away. It was sort of like receiving letters while away at summer camp. In the evenings, I read everyone's comments to Chuck and e-mailed our responses. I became eager to fire off another trip update a few days later in anticipation of receiving e-mails afterward.

E-mails with photos remind one of memorable moments

Take lots of pictures, and then delete most of them. Select between three and five to send with each travel e-mail. More photos make a file too large to send electronically in one e-mail.

Besides, a few images can capture a lot. And of course, written descriptions should expand on what a photo shows, but not repeat it.

Illustrated e-mails are a way of storing memories. Savor them later and live in the moment. When traveling there are always plenty of memorable times.

This Lone Brown Petrel may not have been lonely!

Responses to e-mails provide good feedback

When I described our bird watching trip off the coast of New Zealand, Paul, our birder friend, let me know that the brown petrel who stayed apart from the others probably wasn't an outcast. While the rest of the flock crowded around the chum (block of frozen bird food) on the back of our boat, he kept paddling in circles while making guttural sounds. I had no idea that was typical mating behavior to attract female petrels.

Jim, a retired professional writer, spotted a few typos. The most glaring one was that the Moors built the Mezquita de Cordoba between 800 and 10,000 AD. Oops! It should have been 1,000 AD. He said, "I guess the Moors are still building and will for a looonnnng time!"

Discover what catches people's attention

Readers commented about the face of the kangaroo on a parapet in the town square in Perth, looking away and not facing the crest. In 1923, when the post office was completed, the architect had the kangaroo peering toward the lord mayor's offices because he hadn't been paid.

Our acquaintances wanted to know why a variety of men on a train from Tangier to Fez, kept rotating through our six-person compartment. We figured out that mystery by the time we left the train at Fez. You'll have to read the book to learn why.

Include impressions and quotes

Anyone can obtain travel information, but it's personal encounters that leave a lasting impression. A short, elderly Chinese worker in traditional black garb at our Hong Kong hotel asked us if we were old. He wanted to know our ages, a question we were asked a lot on the trip. When we told him we were from the United States, he covered his face with one hand and sighed. He said, "Why your country have so much trouble?" Then he said, "Big tree with sweets attract many hornets."

What to do with the e-mails after the trip ends

Milk them for gems to use in articles or a book. Treat the e-mail log from your trip with respect by putting it in a binder. Include your trip itinerary.

We asked our daughter to save our trip e-mails for us. Several friends printed them as well. Rereading about those travel adventures brings back memories as I slowly journey ahead turning our adventures into a book about our around-the-world trip.

*Article Photos by Carol Kreis

SCIENCE FICTION–FANTASY

In June of 2018 SWW held a conference for Sci-Fi/Fantasy writers. Members were invited to submit short stories to the *Sage* in advance to raise interest.

Poster Artwork by Rose Marie Kern

RAZZLE FRAZZLE

BY COLIN PATRICK ENNEN

The lazy Sunday afternoon had begun to chafe Razzle Frazz—and the little pup into whose adorable head he'd jammed his consciousness. Of course, his mere presence, semi-ethereal, psychic, from-the-future, was vexing the dog as well, making the poor beast doubly miserable. But Raz refused to feel guilty about this; he *was* on a personally and professionally important anthropological mission, folks. Anyway, like all his blessed species, Shylock would need nothing more than a glance from his master to get his tail wagging, intruder consciousness be damned.

Incidentally, the history books had failed to report the animal's name, this being a rather fuzzy period in the life of its master, the brilliant satirist and speculative fiction writer Colin Patrick Ennen.

It had surprised Raz at first, as the dog was so not...Shylock-y. To him, at least. After all, the last performance he'd seen—on the moon—had put a dolphin-human hybrid in the role. At the same time, he realized, it *would* be just like his favorite early-21st-century author to name a pet after an oft-maligned, perpetually misunderstood (even in the mid-22nd century!) Shakespearean character. Without a hint of pretentiousness, too.

Okay, maybe a little.

Razzle Frazz had entered the dog's mind a few weeks before to observe Mr. Ennen up close, to un-fuzz what was thought to be a crucial period in his artistic development. That was the idea anyway. So far, he'd done a lot of walking around in the balmy Albuquerque winter—good, maybe, if Raz were an archaeo-climatologist. And he'd watched Mr. Ennen stare at a computer screen at great length, the future author honing his scowl, shaking his head, drifting off more times than he could count.

This was important, sure—it showed artistic process and all that. However, Raz had done extensive calculations, given the chrono-gineers a specific destination; he was sure this was when things were supposed to kick off for the author, and he only had a couple of months to hang around. True, Mr. Ennen had, since November, been published three times, including a story considered a classic by Raz's time. But then the author got sick on Christmas, fell off a ladder a week later, and was now contemplating a low-carb meal plan.

"Who writes a book while on a diet?" Razzle Frazz had yelled. Only, given the circumstances, it had come out as a series of howls and woofs. He'd have to talk to the technicians about that.

So, here it was, Sunday, three o'clock, and the guy was staring at the computer screen again, his tongue sticking out of his mouth like a fat pink slug. The keyboard had been silent for close to eight minutes. On the other hand, dude *had* clicked around with the mouse a bunch, but probably only to yet another depressing news article about the current state of the world. Oh, how Raz yearned to assure his hero that everything would turn out; he just had to be patient. But, again, "woof-woof."

That's when the wannabe writer suddenly stopped procrastinating. He sat up straight at his computer, like a string had been pulled from the top of his head, or someone had stuck him in the rear with a thumbtack. Mr. Ennen shook out his hands, winked at his puppy, and started authoring, his tongue creeping ever further from his mouth.

Raz listened to three minutes of furious tapping before he willed the dog to stand and approach his master. Okay, maybe it wasn't ideal to interrupt an artist at work, but they'd told him he couldn't alter history.

Mr. Ennen tore his attention from the screen to address the pup, grinning. "Sup...little fella?" He reached out and caressed Shylock's head, sending a cascade of dopamine shooting through the animal's brain.

Razzle Frazz felt it, too, and knew his body, lying strapped to a table, fixed with countless wires, a century-and-a-half in the future had to be jamming right along.

"Strap in, dude," Mr. Ennen instructed his dog. "This is it." He pointed to the computer screen before returning to work.

Raz directed the dog's eyes up to the glowing square on the table in front of the writer. Another surge of chemical warm-fuzzies coursed through the mutt, this time coming from the brain-intruder.

The dumb bastard had finally started, and Raz would recognize that first paragraph anywhere, anytime.

THE SCOTSMAN'S WIFE

BY SALLY L. KIMBALL

"Excuse me," the fellow museum visitor said. "Do you mind if I press the button?"

Why was I hesitating? It was only a display of a re-enactment of the battle between the Scottish Jacobites and the British Loyalist troops of 1746.

"Does it tell you anywhere what colors represent the Scotsmen?" he asked.

"I'm sorry, I must be blocking your view. I believe it's blue."

The stranger pressed the button. Colored lights flashed. The battle began. My breath caught as the blue lights began to fade. *Which one was my Scotsman?*

When the battle ended, I released a sigh and walked towards the door leading to the battlefield path, a walkway onto the field where men had lost limb or life for their beliefs. Holding the door open, I panicked. "I can't do this," something caused me to say. "I don't want to see the carnage."

Suddenly I heard my spiritual master. "You have the gift to help those poor souls. I understand your human emotions, but you've been directed by the Angelic Masters to help those who died on the battlefield, and still remain earthbound, to make their transition and transmute the negative energy of anger."

You need to set us free. I had heard the spirit voice before my decision to travel to Scotland. Who is "us"? I hesitated, struggling to step upon that hallowed ground for fear I would dishonor the man who had given his life for Scotland's freedom.

Drawn back to the battle display, I felt a presence and glanced toward the battlefield door. My breath caught when waves of energy morphed into the form I recognized as my Highlander husband who had many times appeared in my dreams. His belted plaid and Tartan sash were ripped and covered in blood. His long hair was matted, and his tam and silver bodkin were missing. He stood by the door with his broadsword and Lochaber axe hanging from bloodied hands.

He was my handsome Scotsman, tall and broad with black hair, blue eyes, and muscular arms that had held me close as he whispered love poems in my ear. I closed my eyes and turned my head.

"I pined for you each day, my love," he said. "I walked towards the battlefield with the knowledge I may never hold you close. Then I died on the moors and a thousand more deaths feeling the loss of you as my blood flowed upon the ground. Help my soul cross the veil of time and leave that force that keeps me earthbound. My spirit needs to be free."

I heard my other self say, "Go away, please, I want to remember the day you left for battle." I glanced up and caught his eyes coveting my body. My emotions flamed. "You were my lover and my only love. To see you and then lose you again will be more than I can bear."

His hollow voice tore my heart. "I wanted you to say those words I heard when I walked upon the heather to fight for freedom on that fateful day. *Tighinn air ais dhomh mo ghràdh.*" Come back to me my love.

Tears pooled in my eyes. "I cannot," I whispered. But when I looked at him again, I knew what I had to do. "Please go, my love, to those who wait to help you cross the veil of time. Our souls will be as one again when at last my bonds are freed."

His spirit floated towards me. The bonded spirit of his long-ago wife separated from my body and merged with her lover. Their souls were finally set free.

SCENTS AND PROMISES

BY LISA DURKIN

There he was, a white dog, sitting in the exact middle of the road. Their eyes met, and she had no doubt. He was lost.

Someone was going to hit the little fella, but the last thing she needed was a dog.

She sighed and swerved around him. He watched her with a chin held high despite his bewilderment, and it gave her pause. Noble mustaches beckoned her into a U-turn. It was as if he had a summer cottage in Cornwall and had taken a wrong turn. Someone needed to hear his story.

Beating a tail on the sidewalk, he had moved so she could pull beside him and open the car door. He hopped into the back seat and took his place gazing through heavy brows. She stroked his head and hummed whilst swirling her fingers around his muzzle. At his throat she changed cadence. When she was finished, he said, "I was lost."

"I know." She smiled. Closing the door, she rounded the car and returned to the driver's seat.

"I'm so glad you finally picked me up, because I was SO lost." He placed his feet on the console and asked, "What's your name?"

With a left blinker, she merged into the driving lane. "I'm Judy, and who are you?"

"Rufus."

"Nice to meet you, Rufus." She glanced back expecting him to wag and smile like a regular dog. Rufus peered out the window as if she were his chauffer.

"Where is your collar and why are you so dirty?" She asked.

Rufus gave his leg a lick. "I thought I looked rather dapper."

"And the collar?"

"I'm lost."

Judy scratched her chin. "How did that happen?"

"I don't know, but I can tell you how I got here."

"That will do."

Rufus sat back on his haunches. "This morning, when the dark was over, I was tucked in a ball, and my hair was crisp with frost." His voice lilted. "That's when I smelled sunshine."

"Oh, might you let me see?"

The windshield filled with light. Millions of colors symbolized a spectrum of aromas, an eager world painted by scents and promises.

"I followed a trail where a cat had wandered by. Then there was a hedgehog slumbering in a hole. I didn't stalk the skunk, but I did eat a beef jerky wrapper."

Judy tilted her head. "That will be a problem tomorrow."

"I missed breakfast."

"You don't look like you've missed many meals."

"Isn't that something to be happy about?" Rufus wasn't insulted.

The car hit a pothole. Rufus braced his paws and continued. "There were children giggling, and I found them."

Young voices bubbled through the car speakers. Eager girls vied to pet and preen while ornery boys teased.

"One of them shared a piece of burrito." He smacked his lips. "It stung my mouth, so I found water in a crystal clear stream." Vibrant colors splashed across the windshield. "Ducks were there, and they smelled like feathers and fear. I didn't eat them. I didn't evn chase them."

"You didn't chase the ducks?" She asked.

"No."

Judy was doubtful. "You didn't chase birds?"

Terrified quacking filled the car speakers.

Rufus peered from lowered brows. "I may have startled them a little, but they left their eggs, so I ate them."

"That explains the egg yolk on your beard."

Rufus licked a circle around his mouth. "So where are we going?

"I'm going to take you to a place where your owner can find you, and then you won't be lost anymore." Her voice wasn't very convincing. "You never told me what happened to your collar."

"I remember when The Mom first put it on my neck. It was warm and jangled all the time." An array of color filled the window. "The Daughters hugged and played with me." Little-girl-giggles trilled in the speaker. I stayed there, dark and light, cold and hot, even after The Mom had to trade it for a bigger collar. They fed me breakfast day after day. It was when the leaves were falling that The Mom smelt like worry and there wasn't always enough kibble to fill my tummy. On some nights the house was cold, and sometimes there were no lights in the window. That was when she put things in boxes and carried them away until there wasn't anything but floors and walls."

Judy's car turned and pulled into a parking lot. Fading sunlight glinted off a white, windowless building. Chain-link pens full of huddled dogs lined the property.

"Where are we?" Rufus cocked his head.

"This is where your owner can find you."

"I've been sniffing for her scent and listening for The Daughters' laughter on the wind. The girls haven't hugged me since they left for the bus the morning I got lost. I waited on the itchy mat for The Mother to come out. She hadn't given me breakfast. Her face was angry when the door opened."

A female voice grumbled through the speaker. "Get in the car Rufus."

"I watched the world whirl by through the window until she stopped by the river and let me out. Then she took off my collar and drove away without me. There were so many new aromas. It was fantastic to sniff and track. I got tired, so I patted down a soft spot and slept. That's when I dreamt of you." He climbed into her lap and curled with his nose nestled against her tummy. "I've been looking for you ever since. It was hard, because I didn't know your scent."

A field of colorful swirls filled the window. From deep inside her, Judy knew the spectrum represented her essence. This is what Rufus recognized when their eyes met on the street. There are no coincidences when a dog plants himself in the middle of the road waiting for a particular person in a particular vehicle.

Warmth spread and tingled up her spine.

"You smell like you've been chasing squirrels for too long." Rufus peered at her. "You need a nap."

It wasn't until that instant that she realized how her life, filled with a frenzy of work and family, lacked respite. "That about sums it up."

Rufus yawned. "What happened to your collar?" He asked.

"I was lost, but now you've found me." She put the car in reverse, backed out of the parking lot and headed home with her new friend.

SAGE CHALLENGE:

MEMOIR

Maestro   Photo by Rose Marie Kern

AMBIGUOUS WELCOME

BY MARY THERESE PADBERG

The vast auditorium seemed like a ridiculous place to have a meeting for six new students, but I sat down quietly and waited for the department chair to arrive. I was surrounded by five of my future classmates, all men, only one of whom was familiar since we were in the same orientation group. It had been an overwhelming 24 hours since I had flown cross-country to my new school.

Finally, Dr. Grady entered and walked to the podium below the stage, level with the first row. I hadn't met Dr. Grady yet, but I had spoken to him over the summer when he offered me a small department scholarship for my first year. I was anxious to thank him in person.

After some brief introductions of what the department expected from its math majors he began to take roll. One by one the men around me raised their hands.

"Todd... Enrique... Nathaniel... James... Benjamin."

He scanned the near empty auditorium, avoiding my eye. After an awkward pause he finally asked, "Is there anyone I didn't call?"

Seriously? I thought. *I'm the only girl here so obviously you didn't call my name.*

I raised my hand.

"And you are?"

"Mary Therese Padberg."

He looked at me in shock.

"You don't go to school here."

"What do you mean?" I said. Five faces focused on me making the room feel suddenly crowded.

"How did you get here? Where are you staying?"

I didn't know how to respond and felt nervous under his interrogatory glare.

"I'm staying in McKay Hall."

Dr. Grady balked at my response. His voice grew angry as he said, "How did you get into the dorms?"

"Um, I went to housing and got a key."

"Housing gave you a key? Come with me." Without giving any more of an explanation he dismissed the others and swept me outside.

The salty air swept around me as I followed. I wanted to admire the beautiful palm trees and ocean view surrounding me, but my thoughts were racing. I tried to ask what was wrong, but Dr. Grady was stubbornly avoiding conversation. I wanted to go back to orientation. This was my first opportunity to make friends and I was missing it.

The campus was still foreign to me, but our destination was near. We arrived at the admissions building and Dr. Grady entered the first open door.

"Dr. Grady. How can I help you?"

Ushering me inside Dr. Grady finally explained, "This young lady is not in our records as attending school here but apparently is staying in McKay Hall."

A few more words were exchanged as I stood rooted to the spot. I wasn't listed as a student? How could that be? I had accepted and

122

registered for orientation months ago.

"I'll take care of it."

Dr. Grady left and the man had me sit as he made several phone calls. I couldn't follow much of the conversations, but at last I heard him triumphantly announce "I see" for the last time and hang up the phone.

"Well, Mary," he said. I hated the name Mary. "I've discovered what has happened. Apparently there was an issue with your acceptance reply and it arrived late. As a result, it was sent straight to housing so they could get you placed in the correct orientation weekend and dorm. However, they failed to send the information over to admissions once they were done."

"Okay, so is everything fixed now?"

"Well, not quite. Since we were never informed of your decision to attend we released your financial aid to other students. I can make some calls, but it may not be possible to retrieve your aid package."

He delivered the news calmly, as if he was commenting on the never-changing weather patterns of southern California. I sat there numb, afraid if I tried to respond nothing would come out.

I was miles away from home at a $45,000-a-year institution, a short drive up from Santa Monica with the Hollywood sign visible from the bluff outside, and I was being told my financial aid package was gone. I started doing mental calculations of my bank account: $10 in checking and a little over $200 in savings. I couldn't even afford a flight home!

The man was still talking.

"Why don't you go back to orientation. Try to make friends while I see if there is anything we can do. I'll have someone come get you when I know more."

I nodded and left. I found everyone in that same auditorium, now filled with hundreds of students, watching a skit being performed by our O-leaders. Everyone was laughing and I was on the verge of a breakdown. I couldn't go in.

I wandered the campus looking for a pay phone to call my mom, but when she picked up I broke into tears. Eventually I hung up. Everyone was pouring out of the auditorium and I couldn't avoid my orientation group forever. There was nowhere else to go.

I barely registered the rest of the activities. My efforts were spent trying to stay composed in front of the group. After several draining hours someone finally came to drag me back to admissions.

I was informed that they had called several donors with an emergency plea and as a result my full aid package was restored. While I had lost my opportunity to enjoy orientation and make new friends, I was able to continue as a student at Loyola Marymount University. After my first year of having a patch-work quilt of donors holding my aid together I was adopted by a single donor who generously paid for the rest of my education.

The four years went by rather uneventfully compared to my beginning, but I didn't realize how soon the cycle would repeat itself. Senior year, when applying to graduate school, my University of Iowa acceptance letter was lost in the mail in an ironic twist of déjà vu.

AN UNUSUAL SUITOR

BY BRENDA COLE

A cranky 2-year-old, a purse that refused to stay put and my only free hand clutching the loaded diaper bag. My introduction to the desert that was to become my home was anything, but pleasant. I crossed my fingers that the scenery was greener than it was when I drove through town on vacation when I was 15. Hope died as we walked outside. It was already warm in April, a gritty breeze tried to ruffle my hair as I looked in desperation for familiar vegetation. All the way to the house I intently scanned the trees for Maple, Oak, or Hemlock. Nothing.

We got to the house. Rocks instead of grasses, a scraggly pine and the ever present dusty wind. My husband took our son inside and I tried to get a grip on myself. All my life had been spent on, near or in the water, lots of water. Everywhere I had lived was shades of green with deep black loam beneath it, until now.

I gave myself another mental shake. I gazed about at the multiple shades of brown, tan and rock. Maybe I could finally have a house full of rocks. I seemed to have an entire yard full of them. I turned to get the suitcase when I heard the weirdest noise, a quick clacking. I turned and caught a flash of movement. We had a patio off the bedroom with a four foot tall wall behind the pine. There was something moving on top of the wall. I slowly crept closer and saw it was a strange looking bird. It saw me, stopped, cocked its head then fanned out an enormously long tail and rapidly clicked its beak. Well that explained the sound, then it struck me that it was a road runner!

I had no idea they would be in a city, let alone on my patio wall. I was chuckling to myself about looking for coyotes next and started taking gear into the house. I assumed it would just fly off after a few minutes, but that crazy bird paced up and down for hours. I opened the blinds to show my husband, he was equally astounded. As soon as the bird saw me in the house he hoped off the wall, came up to the closed sliding door and pecked on the glass. I didn't think he could get through them and tried to ignore him. By bedtime he had disappeared, and I wrongly assumed that was the last of him.

As the days went by, I tried to adjust to living in a desert. I learned all about other local fauna. The 6-inch centipede that tried to jump down my shirt when I was dusting the garage shelves met a fitting end, thankfully I have big feet and even larger boots. I even managed to find a coyote, more accurately he found my nice warm driveway and was sunning himself when I came home from work. I had to roll down the window and yell at him to get him out of the driveway.

A month or so after we had moved in I heard a peculiar tapping. I couldn't find anything and realized it was coming from over my head. Our house had clerestory windows in the living room. I looked up, right into the eyes of a roadrunner pecking at the glass. It couldn't be the same one, but I wasn't certain if they were territorial or not. It kept tapping on the glass for a couple of hours.

Every time I looked up, he'd stop. Then when I went back to reading he'd start up again, as if to say, "Hey pay attention to me"!

He kept this up for more than a week. I'd asked around and people at work said maybe he was territorial, he was bored or it was a mating ritual. While the last one sounded far-fetched, I'd heard of similar things before. I just hoped he would get tired and move on.

He disappeared again and then one day I heard a tapping at my front door. I looked out the peep hole and didn't see anyone, maybe it was a delivery. I opened the wood door, looked through the storm door down into the upturned eyes of the roadrunner. He had decided to up his game. He took a step back and looked down at his feet. I followed his gaze and there was a dead, lizard at his feet. OK, mating dance it is.

That was one persistent bird. I spoke, hoping my voice would startle him, no luck. I slammed the door, ignored the lizard and he kept pecking. When my husband got home, he laughed himself silly when I told him about my unusual suitor, until I showed him the dead lizard. Over the next few weeks I would get a tapping at the front door. Lizards seemed a favorite, but I had mice, a snake even a scorpion or two.

I talked to the Ag extension office and after they got done laughing said it should let up come full summer. By August the roadrunner had disappeared. The seasons changed, it got cooler, had some snow and I realized maybe it wasn't so bad down here after all. No 40 below zero temps, I shoved snow with a broom and my Midwestern winter coat never made it out of the closet.

The next spring, I had almost forgotten my suitor and then I heard a tapping above my head. There he was back on my roof, peering down at me. Every spring whenever I see a roadrunner up in the heights I have to smile. I started more new friendships explaining the antics of that misguided avian than I can count, and

I've never been able to watch the roadrunner cartoons again without cheering on my feathered friend.

TORNADO COOKIES

BY JASMINE TRITTEN

Exhausted from sightseeing at the Danish settlement Elk Horn in Iowa, my husband and I arrived late in the afternoon at the Super 8 motel of the small town Clarinda. This was our final destination for the warm June day. After driving for hours amid rolling hills of green cornfields, through high winds and occasional rain squalls, we anticipated relaxing our bodies and clearing our minds in a quiet space.

Dark clouds slowly formed in the bluish-gray sky as we approached the modest motor inn suggesting a downpour at any moment. We hurried into the building with our luggage and checked in at the front desk. Barely had we entered our designated room and thrown our suitcases on top of the king-size bed, when our cell phones began bleeping simultaneously with an unfamiliar alert.

"Jim, look!" I said, staring at my little metal box. Red warning lights lit up. We discovered to our dismay that a tornado was heading straight in our direction. It was only ten miles away. The twister had already touched down on a few houses and pulled up some trees.

"Oh my goodness Jim, how can that be coming out of nowhere?" I exclaimed, gasping for air. "What are we going to do?"

Less than a minute later, the telephone next to our bed rang. I fumbled my way over to answer it as quickly as possible.

"This is the front-desk clerk," the voice on the other end said. "We have an alert. An oncoming tornado is moving in the direction of the motel. For your safety, we urge you and your husband to immediately take shelter inside the laundry room in the central part of the building. It's the safest place."

I thanked her and hung up the phone. After explaining to Jim what she told me, I hollered, "Jim! Come on, hurry up. We must run into the laundry room!" My legs shook. Adrenaline rushed throughout my body. Sirens from outside blasted in my ears with a loud pitch. The intensity of the vibration felt head-splitting. Quickly we dragged our luggage onto the floor and ran for our lives. My heart throbbed. Was this real or something out of a movie?

A scent of clean sheets filled the confined space of the laundry room. Strangers showed up within minutes and crowded the place. Most were men dripping with sweat, maybe from operating the enormous tractors we saw parked nearby. Their body odor polluted the fresh aroma. It was amazing how quickly we all got acquainted with each other in this life threatening situation.

The questions, "Where are you from?" and "How did you land here?" were asked constantly. Claustrophobic, I took a big breath and wondered how long we would be trapped in these tight quarters.

Whoever dared to sneak out of the room reported back to us about intensifying rumbling thunder and constant lightning in the dark sky. Information circulated fast about the latest weather news from the front-lobby television.

At one point, I ventured out of the confined space, only to observe the sky opening up with torrential rain. Hail, the size of marbles, hit the ground. The sound resembled a deafening drum session. I scurried back to the laundry room and told the others what had happened.

A clerk from the front office later informed us that the huge black cloud with a funnel was traveling over our heads. Unpredictable, it might twist and strike down at any given moment. I prayed and visualized us surrounded with white light, the best way I could think of offering protection.

Somebody must have heard my prayers, because the door opened wide, and before us stood the kind clerk from the front desk. In her arms she carried a large plate piled high with freshly baked, chocolate chip cookies, the usual five o'clock treat.

"Tornado cookies," Jim and I yelled at the same time, breaking the silence of a room bursting with anxiety. Our eyes opened wide in anticipation. Just from looking at the mouth-watering, palm-sized saucers oozing with chocolate, I felt my stress melting away. Drool dripped down the sides of my mouth. A heavenly smell emanating from the treats hit my nostrils and overpowered the suffocating body odor.

We all chuckled and then broke into laughter in the midst of the high drama. We stretched our arms out and reached for the miracle food without hesitation. The taste of homemade cookies hypnotized and soothed everyone. Fear left us for the moment. Who cared if we ate too much sugar, and who cared what happened outside? Within minutes, the plate was empty. Warm "fuzzies" helped each of us through the life-endangering experience. "Hurrah for chocolate chip cookies!" we all shouted.

An hour passed before the alarming black cloud moved through the area and dissolved in the sky. No twisting whirlwind damaged our motor inn, although it did touch down and wreak havoc on several houses and fields in the region. On the national news, we later saw the damage. Rooftops were torn off and trees uprooted. Debris flew in all directions.

Luckily, my husband and I had gotten the tornado warning in time. We had survived a possible disaster. The magic of sweet treats helped us to relax through the ordeal. Grateful and thankful, we celebrated our good fortune with a scrumptious dinner at the best restaurant in Clarinda.

1983 Tornado hitting Coronado Mall in Albuquerque.   By Richard Morrow

SCHOOL DAZE(S)

BY LINDA YEN

DARK

To this day I can see the old crone's piercing eyes, her pale, wrinkled face, hear the screech in her voice as she wrenched me from my chair and made me stand.

Next appeared a matron whose crown of curly red hair I remember because I had never seen that color of hair before. There was a gentleness in the way she held me by the shoulders as she spoke to the crone.

But she soon moved away, and I stood, paralyzed by fear, for what seemed an eternity in the assembly room, surrounded by a sea of students and teachers, feeling isolated and humiliated though I had no idea what I was guilty of. This was my initiation into fourth grade in the United States.

Before classes began I had flunked with flying colors a written exam since I neither spoke nor read any English. It was 1956. There were no remedial English courses, no special classes for children of newly arrived immigrants. I was casually left to fend for myself in the regular class.

Maybe my parents and the school officials carried the idea of immersion too far. I don't recall learning much, if anything, that year. Other than the old crone and her icy stare whenever she saw me in assembly hall, I don't recall by name any of the teachers or students.

I do recall the canned prunes we were forced to gulp down for lunch. They looked like snails marking slimy purple trails as I scooted them around the plastic bowl. Perhaps the cafeteria cook was obsessed with constipation. Who wouldn't be constipated from the tasteless fare of rubbery meats and soggy vegetables?

In retrospect, the old crone must have had a notion of loyalty that bordered on lunacy. The red haired teacher brought my younger brother, who apparently fared better than I, to explain to me in Chinese that I must stand, place my hand on my chest, and sing the patriotic song.

I told him I was born Chinese, and would never sing songs to any other country. But then, not wishing to be terrorized any longer, I grudgingly complied. After the mandatory mouthing of "My Country 'Tis of Thee," the old crone made all the students dance the minuet. Upon noticing that I rose obediently for the singing, she directed a young boy to escort me to the dance floor.

I dragged my feet, wanting to escape the bizarre charade. Why would an American public institution celebrate an archaic European dance during grade school lunch hour? The crone must have had more than one screw loose. Perhaps she believed she descended from European royalty. Perhaps she thought she was Marie Antoinette. Too bad the schoolyard wasn't equipped with a guillotine.

I was too young and naïve to come up with more twisted motives. It was, after all, the fifties. Maybe she thought I was Japanese and my family should have remained in the internment camps. Maybe she thought I was a spy from North Korea or, worse yet, an agent provocateur for the Communists and labor unions.

LIGHT

Mr. Heineman blinked and almost tripped when he entered our sixth grade classroom. "Surprise!" we shouted as we leapt from our crouched positions behind our desks. After he realized what we had done, he moved to the middle of the room and sat down on a student's desk.

With a sigh, he removed his dark rimmed glasses. "Oh you guys," he said, wiping away the tears in his eyes. The class huddled around him for a hushed second, then broke out in giggles and joyful laughter.

One does not need to understand a person's words to sense the kindness in a smile or a nod. The spoken word is defined by the culture that generated it, while the language of the heart is universal. Mr. Heineman guided us, not simply with words, but with his heart.

His face lit up like a proud parent whenever we accomplished a task, however small and insignificant in the scheme of things. He gave us hope and encouragement so that, by the end of the school year, each one of us went home convinced that we possessed a particular gift, despite the fact that we had been relegated to the "slow learners" class.

We were a mongrel lot. The classmates I recall were Annabelle, a tall Swedish girl with long blonde braids; Annette, a petite, pretty Puerto Rican who wore low cut tops to show off her budding breasts; Roberto, an Italian kid with a shy, radiant smile; Sam, a pockmark faced Anglo boy who was slow as a tortoise, but would eventually reply to a question. Though we each had an idiosyncratic way of expressing ourselves in English, we had no difficulty understanding one another.

Class began with Mr. Heineman explaining the day's lesson on the blackboard. Later, he'd stop by our desks to check our progress. He stooped down next to me when he noticed that I had completed a long division problem. "What a genius!" he exclaimed. I lapped up the compliment but knew better. By the time I had completed third grade in Taiwan's regimented, learn-by-rote Chinese school, I already knew decimals and fractions. I was relieved, though, that my sixth grade textbook did not go beyond long division. It meant being spared from doing any more math homework.

Mr. Heineman swept the cobwebs from our minds by taking us out of the classroom. We'd scamper across a grassy knoll in Central Park, lugging crayons, paper pads, and lunchboxes, to settle down and draw the fall foliage. We strolled, wide eyed, mouths agape, past gigantic displays of dinosaur skeletons in the Museum of Natural History. We emboldened ourselves to dream under a wide canopy sky as we traveled to distant planets, comets, and stars at the Planetarium.

For the final day of class, Annette, a natural team leader, suggested we throw him a surprise party. We pooled our resources, blew balloons, taped them on the walls alongside streamers made of supple construction paper, and cobbled together a farewell poster bearing each of our signatures. It was the last time I'd see Mr. Heineman or my fellow classmates. That day I watched a grown man weep, and learned, without need of words, the meaning of gratitude.

THE SLIPPERY SLOPE

BY EVELYN NEIL

Walt moved into the downstairs bedroom last night, downstairs to sleep in the new Select Comfort bed. The head could be raised to ease his breathing difficulties caused by advanced emphysema. The foot, when elevated, relieved the swelling in his ankles and took the pressure off his arthritis-racked lower back. The nights of the previous month had been spent trying to sleep propped up on pillows. Being flat, even with the assist of three liters of oxygen, gave him a drowning sensation.

Surrounded by pillows, I was left alone to toss and turn in the cold king-sized bed in the master bedroom upstairs where we had slept, made love and talked our way through more than fifty-eight years. Staring wide eyed into the inky darkness surrounded by deafening silence, I realized how dependent I'd become on the white noise of the oxygen concentrator and Walt's snoring to lull me to sleep. The worst kind of loneliness gripped me.

Barely breathing, I listened for sounds of the night. Sounds I rarely noticed, the pyracantha branches scraping across the stucco, pine cones scurrying across the roof in an attempt to outrun the wind, coyotes yipping and barking in celebration of a newly harvested meal. Our life together was being whittled away one piece at a time. Like a slow amputation with no anesthesia.

The high-tech bed with the remote control was an immediate hit with Walt. Everyone who came to the house, including the young man who came to wash the windows, was dragged downstairs for show and tell.

"See, it has a blue night light underneath the bed that shines out the sides. This button on the remote turns on the bedside lamp." Walt demonstrated. "Here, lie down. Feel the massage. Do you want full body, lower body, upper body or wave?"

Walt assured me he was sleeping better. "And," he said. "I don't have to climb those damned stairs to go to bed or to use the bathroom. I can watch my movies here in the den any time of day or night."

But for all this, he still retained fluid. His skin stretched ever tighter over his expanding belly. His once slender legs looked like shapeless stumps.

I finally persuaded him to see his long-time cardiologist, Bob Gray, the savior who'd performed the angiogram and angioplasty procedures in 1991 following the first heart attack. He oversaw Walt's recovery following bypass surgery and threaded stents into his clogged arteries after each subsequent heart attack in 2000, 2006 and 2011. Not only was he Walt's doctor, but his friend. He had three of Walt's framed photos of Antelope Canyon on display in his office.

Brightly-colored hot air balloons hovered in the cobalt sky over brilliant gold cottonwoods along the Rio Grande the first week of October when we travelled to the north valley for Walt's appointment with Dr. Gray.

Heather, the nurse, escorted us to an examining room, weighed Walt and took his vitals. Following a short wait the doctor entered the room.

"Well, old buddy, it is what it is, the beginning of congestive heart failure." Dr. Gray patted Walt's arm. "Your lungs aren't supplying your heart with the oxygen it needs. Your body is retaining fluid." The doctor sat on a stool in front of Walt. "I can only imagine you feel like your head's in a bucket of water."

I grasped Walt's hand. Neither of us spoke. We'd begun the long slide down a slippery slope.

Finally, Walt, who never let bad news interfere with his zest for life, stood and leaned on his cane, "Doc, I wish you could have seen the deer at our water trough this morning. Two does with five spotted fawns."

"Five babies from two females?"

"Yeah, one had twins, the other triplets."

Dr. Gray buttoned Walt's blue Pendleton shirt, pulled up his suspenders and put his arm around his shoulder. "You're going to be fine, my friend. Mind your diet. Put your feet up and enjoy your deer."

Walt adjusted the shoulder strap on his oxygen bottle and shifted his cane. "Come, sweetheart, let's go to the Daily Grind. A Chicken Panini would taste good about now."

I walked slowly by my husband's side and held the door while he made his way painfully out of the doctor's office to our car. After helping him into the passenger seat and hooking his seat belt, I settled behind the wheel, fastened my seat belt and adjusted the rear-view mirror. What day had I become the driver?

ROMANCE

Artwork by Joanne S. Bodin

FOREVER LOVE

BY DONALD DENOON

Our dream began that day we met
A place and time we'll not forget

You smiled at me, your eyes did too
And then you saw me smile at you

Across the room we could not speak
So I stepped out a path to seek

The crowd was vast and I pushed on
To where you were, but you were gone

How could it be? I looked again
At empty space where you had been

And then I looked where I had been
And saw you there with playful grin

You mouthed the words *Please stay right there*
I did not move, I did not dare

With warm hello you greeted me
And I responded nervously

Hello, I stayed at your command
You grinned at me and took my hand

We hit it off that day we met
And glory be! We have "it" yet

At times we fight or disagree
And state our cases mightily

But we've found ways to stay together
Through stormy days and sunny weather

And now today with loved ones near
We say *I do* with voices clear

And clasp our hands as outward sign
That we are blessed with Love Divine

Our dream began that day we met
A place and time we'll not forget

This love of ours, a dream come true
Forever me with forever you

To Nick & Victor – June 10, 2017

THE LANTERN

BY HARULE STOKES

Darkness filled my hollow core for such a long time I'd forgotten what light felt like. I could no longer find memories of warm illumination, could no longer feel it lift my spirit on dark days. I sat in that darkness and remained ignorant of what life felt like to exist in anything but the shadows. That space became my home and I learned to not only endure it, but enjoy my stay therein. It was safe in the gloom, because I knew it. I mastered my navigation within its rocky seas, accepting the crashes, satisfied only with the fact they didn't shatter me.

Everything changed when I saw the light.

There it stood, defiant before the shade, inscrutable to it and subsequently, myself. How could such a thing exist in the midst of this army of night? How could it beam its warmth, give it away so freely, and not be consumed by it? How could this light pass so easily through the moonless landscape and never be marred or dimmed by the roughened environment? Yet, there it stood, joyfully giving its energy to the world with a bright smile and a sunny disposition. Then, the light smiled at me.

I wanted the light for myself.

When you see the light, know of its presence, you are forever changed. No longer can you be satisfied with the cold shadows. Once you desire the light, it becomes impossible to be at peace within the night's grasp or satiated by its muted existence. You can only seek the light once entranced. So, with greed in my heart, I moved to take the light, contain it. I wanted to shackle the light and consume it for my own desire, needed to be its sole possessor. To my great surprise, the light, seeing me through a world of darkness, sought to give its light to me willingly. The light wanted a home.

I cannot contain the light.

Too big to be locked away, too powerful to be enclosed within my grasp, I feared I might lose the light to the shattered shadows of desired hopes that lived within me. But, wanting to contain the light... that's a fool dream. Nothing can control the light. It cannot be forced into a box and sealed away. It cannot be confined and held back from the world. I dreamed that dream for a time until I saw the truth through the illumination the light brought with its mere presence. It showed me my true desire. I didn't want to only contain the light, I wanted to be it. But, I cannot be the light. I cannot steal the light's power or draw from the warmth it gives, a sense of power. That is not my role.

I am the lantern.

I protect the light with my love. Through the windows of my soul, filled with my love for the light, its warm glow can shine even brighter. I am the lantern, not the light. Through the love I give with my willingness to fulfill my purpose, the light can illuminate the night, guide the lost to safe shores and chase away the chill of darkness. I know this to be true, because the light performed this service for me.

Today, the light and the lantern are one. Together, we can do great things. That is OUR purpose. That is why we have one another. That is why we were married. So, I am forever thankful for your light, for you have given me a profound reason to love.

Rio Grande Gorge Photo by Rose Marie Kern

UNREQUITED

BY AUDREY HANSEN

By the time he neared the canyon, the wind had pumped up to a moderate gale. A daunting impediment to some, perhaps, but he merely jabbed his feet deeper into the sandy trail and met the gusts head-on.

From time to time he threw back his head, exhilarated. He opened his arms to the sky. *God he loved this path, the freedom of this space.*

He came to the arroyo, trotted down one side and up the other. The, there *she* was again – her long blonde hair blowing under a blue denim hat. She kept an easy pace beside a gray and tan dog – Australian Shepherd, probably.

He wouldn't, couldn't, wait for another time.

"Hey!" He raised his voice. "Hey, wait up." He increased his speed until he was jogging at her side. "I've seen you every morning around this time for more than two weeks now. Live near here?"

She didn't turn her head and maintained her same effortless stride.

"Hey, I don't mean to be too familiar or anything, just that I've see you so often. Been running this trail long?"

At last, she looked at him. "Oh, sorry. My mind was elsewhere, I guess."

He smiled. "You didn't answer my questions."

She slowed to a walk, reining in the dog. She changed the leash to her other hand to put the dog between her and the jogger. The dog stopped abruptly, tugged at its chain and tried a leap at this intruder. A low, menacing growl rose from its throat.

She didn't look at the dog, just tightened her grip. The dog barked twice, straining at the leash.

"Hey, get some control of that dog."

"Dusty protects me," she said.

"Yeah, from what?"

"Oh, whatever..." she said.

"Well, keep a good grip on him."

"What do you want?"

"Just wanted to say 'hello'...to meet you actually. You married or something?"

She looked away and briefly closed her eyes, tight. "No. No, I guess not."

"You *guess* not?"

"Stuart and I used to walk this trail every morning, together."

"Stuart?"

"Oh, my husband. He died a few months ago."

"Gee. I'm sorry."

She started a slow job, still holding the dog close.

"Hey, wait. Would you like to have coffee later? After your run?" He matched her stride.

"No, Stuart wouldn't like it."

"*Stuart* wouldn't like it?"

"I can't have another friend. It's just Stuart, me and Dusty here...forever."

He stopped. "What?"

She went on.

"Goodbye." She said.

For a moment he stood watcher her, then turned back. He would find another trail. He picke dup his pace.

Once he looked over his shoulder and watched her blonde hair blowing the the wind in the distance. The dog, on a longer rein now, ran carefree through the low brush at the side of the trail.

Crazy woman... He picked up a handful of sand and threw it into the wind.

SAGE CHALLENGE

DESERT STORIES

High Desert Trail   Photo by Rose Marie Kern

HIGH DESERT

BY GAYLE LAURADUNN

In hot windblown sun
my gravel yard yields freckled
milk-vetch of pink-purple
petals or dandelions of brightest yellow
sprouted from grains of sand spread thin
beneath all that is left in this high

desert where once an ocean broke
waves. The neighbor's mulberry tree
spreads its roots to search for water.
Runners creep between volcanic
glass laid down long ago
by the diminished peaks across
the Rio Grande. The foundation cracks.

The house shifts. The owners pack
and steal into the night cursing
the tree. It acquiesces. Becomes
a stump hacked to pieces, composted
to earthworms.

LAST NIGHT IN THE KALIHARI

BY NATHAN MCKENZIE

Sun set late over the Kalahari in mid-January. Still, he didn't mind it on this evening as it would be marking the start of his last night. For the past eight months he'd lived in a little tent on the sand encrusted banks of what had once been Lake Makgadikgadi. He'd been awarded a grant the year before to study the life cycle of the Bushman Beetle. Though his research wasn't complete, the grant had come to an end.

He'd received word by mail two weeks prior that his replacement would be Dr. Jordan Peterson out of UCLA. He'd never met Dr. Peterson and never seen him speak at conference, but he had read one of his papers for the American Coleopterists Society and had been impressed. He dreaded going back, but was thankful that someone so well regarded would be continuing his work.

As the moon rose into view overhead he decided to lay his bedroll outside and enjoy the stars for one last night. The Kalahari is one of the great ecoregions of Africa. Unlike its sister to the North, the infinitely more famous Sahara, the Kalahari is actually only a semi-desert and can thus play host to a variety of different plants and animals who enjoy its arid climate.

Since June he too was one of its inhabitants. His schedule included weekly trips in his rented Jeep to a small village 40 miles up the road where he would purchase fresh supplies and stop by the post office to mail or receive any correspondence. It was how he learned of Dr. Peterson; it was also how he received the last letter from his wife.

"I'm sorry." Was the ominous opening sentence of the letter, two little words that said so much. She went on to tell him how isolated she felt over the past year, how clear it was to her that their marriage had failed even if he couldn't see it and she was tired of trying. She told him that she'd met someone and decided to move on. Of course, she was "so sorry" but that's just the way things were.

He didn't cry when he read it, he had anticipated the letters arrival for months. The marriage hadn't ended the day she wrote the letter, it hadn't even ended when he made the decision to come to the Kalahari, so many months before. The marriage had ended the day Allison died.

Allison was only three. She'd been born with a hole in her heart and a sense that life would not be long. The doctors did all they could initially. Operations were performed and lifestyle adjustments were prescribed, but such remedial efforts rarely equate to miracle. She died on a Tuesday afternoon. At the time she was playing quietly in her room when she began to cough. The coughs began innocently enough but gradually worsened. Paramedics were called, as they'd been called so many times before, and arrived 15 minutes later. By that time she was choking audibly. He held her feeble body as they administered oxygen and checked her pulse but was ushered out of the way when her wheezing began. He wasn't there at those last moments of her life, when her lips turned white then blue and her pulse flattened out. He couldn't bring himself to look on.

Everything changed after that. He and his wife slept in separate beds in separate rooms. They had meals separately and kept separate schedules. It wasn't a matter of blame or misplaced anger; it was that their styles of grief were so different. He threw himself into his work while she inhabited a world of memories; combing through photo albums and pulling out every little article of Allison's clothing, caressing every little sock. When the opportunity came for him to travel to Africa to do extended research he took it. It was wrong of him, he knew, to leave her alone in her grief, but the walls of their house seemed to crowd in around him, pressing down on him till he nearly forgot how to breathe. He saw the trip as an escape.

He wondered what it would be like to return to it now. The house would be empty this time. The pictures that lined the walls would have been removed, leaving yellow sun stains in their place. Allison's room would be emptied out. Perhaps he could get an apartment near the University and try to start all over. All he could do was try. . .

* * *

The sound of a jeep making its way over the plain to his camp sight woke him. He unzipped his bedroll, stood up and watched as the vehicle neared his tent and finally stopped beside his own jeep. From behind the wheel, out stepped a woman of slight build with brown hair and dark sunglasses. She was wearing a black tank top, white over shirt and cargo capris.

"Hi, I'm Jordan Peterson," she said, extending her hand and smiling

He shook her hand gently, "Nice to meet you."

"Not what you were expecting?" She laughed, looking at the surprised expression on his face. "I get that all the time."

He nodded and laughed. "I hope you like it here as much as I have."

"I hope so," she said pausing for a moment. "You've done good work out here. I know you applied for an extension with the committee and were denied. But I'm gonna need some help finishing this work in the next few months. I told them that and they agreed to let you stay on if you want. "

"Ok," He said smiling.

"I mean, you'll have to work with me. I hope that won't be a problem."

"I'll manage," he said. She laughed at him then, a great belly laugh, then inhaled and throwing her hands behind her head turned around and stared out at the Kalihari.

RESONANCE

BY DINO DE LEYBA

I am the eagle's nest, the color
of your skin, the white and blue
of the eyes that see you. I am
the volcano, the lava that flows
from the fire within. I am tears
from the sky, the rain most unexpected.
I am the roadrunner, the lizard,
the hot sun, the cracked mud of the
riverbed. I am the turquoise sky,
the pink reflection of your setting sun.
I am the Native American dance that
echoes on the banks of the Rio Grande. I am
the displaced child on the street corner,
the prayer left in the cathedral. I am
the cactus bloom, symbolic of your
answered prayer. I am this great land,
the joy in your desire to live, a new
day. I am the face of the desert.

Abandoned Barn   Photo by Rose Marie Kern

DESERT DANGERS

BY ELAINE CARSON MONTAGUE AND GARY TED MONTAGUE

I pedaled hard to haul a couple of squarish two-gallon cans of water on a little platform with two-inch sides. After several trips on my trike through the weeds to the hog pens, I was sweating. The sun threatened to blister my six-year-old neck just as I heard a rattle and ran, screeching, "Snake! Rattlesnake! Dad, come quick."

He hunted for the snake in overgrown weeds. Sure enough, he found that reptile and killed it with a hoe. After that, I stayed away from dangerous, thick weeds where I could not see what was hiding unless Dad went ahead of me, and we carried buckets of water.

Sometimes a cold snap was followed by hot, dry wind. Stony grains bit my face and neck while Dad cut feed and piled it into a big wagon during harvest. I was too young to help much and begged him to let me ride atop the bundles. He gave me a hand. My bottom jostled from side to side, and I was frightened I might fall onto a lurking slitherer.

Farming was hard on dry land, which is much different from having irrigation. Dad cultivated, selected seed, and timed the tilling or listing, planting, and weeding to conserve every drop of sparse rain that fell in arid New Mexico. Our crops included sugar cane and sorghum grains like hegari, maize, and calfer corn. We thrashed them to retrieve grain to feed horses, cows, chickens, and pigs. Once we harvested the grain, the combine collected and bound the stalks into bundles, which we left standing to cure. When they were dry, we hauled them by wagon to a location where we had placed a tractor with a feed grinder. Watching for hidden snakes, we fed stalks by hand into the grinding machine. Out came ground silage for cow feed. We stored silage in holes in the ground or in silos above ground where the feed fermented and became animal food, or fodder.

We spit out grit carried by hot wind in need of a drink and prayed for moisture on our 360-acre farm. Sporadic, welcome downpours sometimes turned on us and caused flash floods that drowned half-grown crops. The muck caked my shoes and hardened the ground into treacherous ruts. New plantings or weeks of work washed out. The cost was high because of wasted seed and time. Sometimes it was too late to start over. When that happened, life was squeezed out of us. We needed everything we planted. But when a rainbow stretched across the sky after one of those devastating storms, Mom reminded us that it was God's promise to love us always. So, we tried again.

The year of my first summer home from the New Mexico School for the Blind was extra dry. I was nine, had low vision, and was happy to be home for the summer. I missed working on projects like the lean-to shed Dad built to protect the animals from bad weather and the corrals of crossties discarded by the railroad. On a day in August, Sis, Mom, Dad, and I sang as we drove back from shopping. It was a glorious day. We topped a little rise. Our world came to a standstill.

"Smoke, Dad. Look." Mom said, pointing out the window.

"Good God! The whole place is on fire." He hit the gas.

My heart jumped in panic at his cry, and Sis leaned across me to stick her head out my window. I could smell smoke before we jumped out of the car. My eyes stung. What if our house were in ruins? Were the animals hurt? Men ran around throwing water at the flames. We joined them, grabbed buckets, dunked them in the horse trough, and attacked the inferno. It was too late. We watched helplessly as the fire devoured outbuildings and turned corrals to ash. Thankfully, the men had freed the animals. That day I learned neighbors could depend on each other.

"Sorry we couldn't do more," the men said as they slapped Dad's back.

"That's all right. You kept us from losing everything. I hate seeing the horses scorched, but none of our animals died because you boys let them go."

"We found your gate open but didn't see nobody."

"I figure the fire started when someone came acrost our proppitty to get to Monument Rock along old Route 66. They can't resist its ice-cream cone shape. Things like this happen, but I al'us loved this life. I'll get to rebuilding tomorrow."

The fire might have started with a spark off a train or a pickup's exhaust or when a careless hobo passing through flicked a cigarette into the brush. We never knew for sure.

The house was safe. We almost forgot why we had been so happy coming home from shopping. It was the day we had victory in Japan, VJ Day. World War II was over. We had danced with people on the streets and shouted the news, so everybody knew. Everyone hugged and kissed and hollered, "Thank you, God! Our boys are coming home!" and "No more rationing!"

The horns blasted, and church bells pealed as we laughed. Sis and I jumped up and down and ran to tell whoever we saw.

Mom clapped her hands, "My brothers will be coming home."

Dad bought Cokes and ice cream cones to celebrate. That's why we sang in the car till we got to the rise.

The big war had ended, but we had our own battle to fight. It was time for me to go back to school. I thought of all the work Dad had ahead of him and was sorry I would not be at home to clean up and rebuild. I knew that next Christmas I would find new corrals and another barn Dad's two hands had built.

MOJAVE MIND

BY SAM MOORMAN

Truly in deserts
nothing is beautiful
and so very still
everything quiets

Sweat drains your mind
of chemicals until
you muse truly
on life here and after

You work spooling barb wire
and pulling wood posts
to undo a cattle fence
no longer needed

Mindful only
of fragrant sage
cat-claw brush
and cactus thorns

WRITERS UNBOUND

SWW members are always invited to submit articles, essays, stories and poems whether there is a monthly theme or not. One of the stories is a review of one of the many classes held by SWW, this one highlights author Melody Groves' class on writing for magazines. One discusses an option for the writer's bane – carpal tunnel syndrome, and there are some delightful pieces involving pets. Here are some of the jewels sent to the *Sage*.

ON THE VIRTUES OF SESQUIPEDALIANISM

BY STAN RHINE

Imagine that you are ensconced in your comfortable reading chair, an icy glass of your favorite hot-weather libation at your elbow. A book lies open in your hands. The author has reached up from its pages to ensnare you and draw you into the tale. The soothing piano concerto playing softly in the background has receded to inaudibility. You have been totally captivated by the power, the charm, the mesmerizing quality of the printed word.

Then an unfamiliar word viciously derails your train of thought. You screech to a halt. What do you do? Snarl and throw the @#$% book against the wall? Calmly put it down and resolve to initiate a small celebration upon hearing of the author's death? Make a mental note never again to buy anything written by that uppity so-and-so?

We are repeatedly warned of the hazards of tossing alien words at our readers. The compositional disciplinarians, those Gurus of

Grammar, Strunk and White, devote two pages to the exposition of their Fourteenth Commandment, "Avoid Fancy Words." Contemporary scolds, such as Gary Provost, in his *100 Ways To Improve Your Writing*, says, "A word that your reader doesn't recognize has no power. If it confuses the reader and sends him or her scurrying for the dictionary, it has broken the reader's spell (p74)."

But is breaking the reader's spell a cardinal sin? Can a spell once broken never be mended? Is an author's hold on a reader really so tenuous as that? Nonsense. Opportunity lost. You could at least try to sound the word out, breaking it down into its constituent elements, *sesqui-pedal.* I know a fellow who keeps a dictionary next to his reading chair. He is always delighted when he stumbles across an exotic word. He leafs through the dictionary, occasionally being diverted to graze on a succulent word or two on the way. Finally, he arrives at the target word, reads the definition, ponders it, and returns, enriched, to the book.

Shameful! you say, to interrupt a pleasant read with a dictionary detour. But don't you admire an author who is so concerned with trying to convey just exactly the right meaning that he interrupts his or her writing to search for the one word that best does so? Sure, you can glean something of the author's intent from context, but isn't it better to discover exactly what the author meant, wallowing in all of the word's delicate shadings and nuances? Think how much richer your reading experience becomes if you traipse down the occasional shady-looking linguistic byway into the unknown.

However, writing advice is invariably *keep it simple*. Hemingway is extolled for his use of simple words; "Look," they coo, "nothing over two syllables." Nice, fat, expressive words like BOOM! a fine onomatopoetic word that seems to beg for an exclamation point! Or, take "bust." No, pay attention—this is bust, as in to go broke.

Together those two words give us that pithy, three-syllable capsule history of mining in the western United States; the inevitable cycle of **boom and bust**.

It may be a bit hackneyed, but it is monosyllabic.

On occasion, though, don't we long for something a bit meatier, something that will leave a savoriness to linger in our neuronal networks? Something that will bring an admiring smile to our lips? Something, say, a bit more sesquipedalian? Bon vivant, traveler and history-dilator, Lucius Beebe, inhabited his own flowery writing style, one that reeked with fragrances of the 19th century. Beebe, moreover, was never one to settle for the merely immense word when he could employ the Brobdingnagian. In his writing on the history of Nevada, the mundane "boom and bust" metamorphosed into the Beebean polysyllabically alliterative "Bonanza and Borrasca."

Now we all know what a bonanza is. It may lack the punch of boom, but "bonanza" sparkles with the allure of gold—a quick buck, a spectacular windfall. What of Borrasca? From the context, we can tell that it is bad. But to stop there denies us an understanding of the richness of the word. Random House says that "borrasca" is a variant of borasca, a squall (especially in the Mediterranean), usually accompanied by thunder and lightning. The word may even have its roots in *Boreas*, the north wind. A borasca is thus no fun. It is ugly and unpleasant—but the word transports you—you lean into the screaming gale, buckling your oilskin coat tightly about you, mashing your dripping rain hat down firmly on your head and lashing yourself to the mast to keep from being swept overboard by the roiling sea, whipped to a froth by the howling borasca.

So there you are—borrasca is literally stormy weather, far more poetic and literary than the monosyllabic "bust." Why settle for three syllables when you can have seven? Especially if you can get paid by the syllable.

Oh, yes, sesquipedalian. We can chop this seemingly daunting word in half, giving us sesqui and pedal. Sesqui is from the Latin, meaning one-and-one-half, as in sesqui-centennial, or a century-and-a-half. Pedal is Latin for foot. The literal meaning of the word is, therefore, a foot and a half, while the literary meaning is a propensity to choose (foot-and-a half) long words.

Yes, the advice to writers is to use short words. There are scores of them, simple, direct, easy to understand. But brains, like muscles, hypertrophy with use. Consider, if you will, practicing the rarely acknowledged virtues of sesquipedalianism.

PS: Isn't there something deliciously oxymoronic about the 5-syllable sesquipedalian word "monosyllabic?"

TO WRITE BETTER, DRAW BADLY

BY KATHY LOUISE SCHUIT

My mother always painted. As kids, wherever Mom took us, she also brought canvas, easel, a wooden paints box, and the scent of linseed oil. She painted while we swam, she painted while we learned to play instruments, she painted when we misbehaved and she couldn't take it any longer.

But she never shared this passion with us. Painting was hers and hers alone. After Mom passed away, her brushes, palette knives and pencils became mine. I had no idea what to do with them.

By age 12, I had decided I could be a writer but any drawing talent I might have possessed never matured past the stage of a three-year-old with a crayon.

Still, holding on to that connection with my mother, I suddenly wanted to learn to draw.

Obviously, I needed help.

I turned to Amazon. My "learning to draw" search rewarded me with several prospects; the one that spoke to me was Betty Edwards – *Drawing on the Right Side of the Brain.* She had my attention at the Introduction, where she says, "The course is designed for persons who cannot draw at all, who feel they have no talent for drawing, and who believe that they can never learn to draw." Yep. That's me.

According to Betty, I didn't need to learn the rules of drawing so much as to re-learn how to notice the world around me.

I was free to break rules I didn't even know, to just have fun, to remember the smell of linseed oil.

I embarked on drawing with zero thoughts of acquiring fame, fortune or even the approval of my family for anything I drew. I knew my depictions lacked form or style, but it pleased me to make them and that's all I expected.

Months later, struggling with a novel that I'd been working on with a friend, I decided to stop trying to sort out how to get just the *right* the words on paper and to draw instead.

My mind quieted. It wandered. It played with ideas, ideas for the sunflower petals forming under my fingers, ideas for dinner, ideas for the novel...

The exact words I needed for the novel flooded into my mind.

Having had past experience with sudden bursts of brilliance (usually while driving) I knew how quickly they can disappear back to the mysterious place from whence they come so I didn't waste time looking for a real pencil. Instead, I tightened my grip on the fat charcoal stick in my hand and started writing.

The sunflower disappeared under a torrent of words. I flipped the page over and filled it. I pulled out another sheet of drawing paper, then another. In fifteen minutes, the chapter I'd been struggling with for weeks was finished. It didn't have commas or periods or, for that matter, capitals. For possibly the first time in my life, I didn't care. I liked it. That's all that mattered.

This was revelation!

The Editor/Critic we all know so well has always had strong

claws in me, but I've fought back. My copies of Natalie Goldberg – *Writing Down the Bones* and *Wild Mind,* and Anne Lamott – *Bird By Bird,* are so dogeared that the poor, torn-off corners now just serve as pointy bookmarks.

I am ever grateful to these brilliant writers for sharing their processes with me, but now I think that, until I read Betty Edwards' book and tried to draw, I could never truly set my mind aside so my self could create.

My new writing process starts with drawing. This exercise reminds me that all I need to do to write well is give up everything I think I know about writing well. With more drawing practice, I hope to eventually let go of sentence structure, to never again feel that prickly *there's a preposition at the end of a sentence* sensation, to write with more consideration for my characters than for commas, to regain the wonder for the world that I had when I was three and to write what makes me happy...with crayons.

Artwork by Kathy Louise Shuit

SOMETIMES I NEED THE DISTANCE

BY ARLENE HOYT-SCHULZE

Sometimes I need the distance
to hide my heart...

But what does it know if alone?
A lone heart, a stillness makes,
its way unto foreign shores.

A mooring there, alone and still,
a set of footsteps cross
loud or soft, I know not which
for alone their steps they make.

I pause, I hesitate to look back
as the whole story is told
verse by verse, then and there,

Hope's dream held in each solitary breath
cool from the storm, steam
forms from each deep breath...

How are we to know then,
this breath which speaks no words,
yet holds life's narrative in its wake?

To hold that breath...
the one... that wakes and stirs
and breathes in life,
returning passion
expressed and shared....

that one breath that bears life's
dreams ... aspiring birth.

MASSAGE FOR CARPAL TUNNEL SYNDROME

BY JENNIFER BLACK

"Just amputate my right arm," Joe said.

The spunk in his eighty-year-old eyes dares me to question him as he lay on the massage table. I'm around half his age, and finally smart enough to keep quiet and listen. He points to the top of his arm. "Just take it from here. There's pain down to my first three fingers. Burning. Tingling. Numbness. It's a package deal, so take it all." With the assistance of WebMD, Joe self-diagnosed carpal tunnel syndrome (CTS). Is there anything I can do?

As a medical massage therapist, I encounter people who are at their wits' end over the discomfort they endure. That, along with the disruption it causes to their quality of life, is usually what leads them to my office. Joe experiences symptoms with certain arm movements and activities: typing at the computer, brushing his hair, and using a can opener, to name a few. Without making eye contact, he reveals that he quit the stretching exercises I gave him two weeks ago. I could smile and nod, but his eyes are still closed, so I accept his confession with a placid face. He continues on about how the pain wakes him at night, and blames it on his curled hand-to-chest position when side-sleeping.

I massage his forearm. "If you see your doctor, she'd help you with that. In the meantime, does lying on your back help?"

"Yes, but you see, I'm asleep. The only time I know I've changed positions is when I wake up. And at night--"

When I apply pressure to a small knot in his forearm, he interrupts himself,

"I feel that in the palm of my hand. If you could just cut my skin and peel it off, you'd see what's going on."

Since I don't have X-ray vision yet, and am not licensed to cut into him, I question him about his culinary experience. Has he ever prepared raw chicken? Yes. Does he remember seeing a white film between the skin and muscle? Yes.

Well, humans are designed the same way. That white film is called fascia. It runs throughout the body without interruption and exerts up to 2,000 pounds of pressure per square inch. Fascia wraps around muscle fibers, individual muscles, muscle groups, and organs, and sometimes ratchets everything it encases. If we can affect the consistency of the fascia, systemic change occurs.

Even though he knows the drill, I give Joe the how-massage-works-spiel, but tailor it to his current situation: massage releases tight muscles, especially on the underside of the forearm so tendons take up less space as they pass through the carpal tunnel. Blood and lymph circulation increase, which promotes healing. Inflammation and pain decrease. Massage along the path of the median nerve releases it from muscle entrapment. If scar tissue is present, it's remodeled. But sometimes, the pathology of CTS progresses beyond the conservative reach of massage, and surgery is a common remedy. However, amputation is regularly omitted from the treatment plan.

CTS is often created and exacerbated by repetitive motion, so one of the first recommendations to decrease symptoms is to quit the offending activity. Joe assures me he'll continue typing. In that case, go see the doctor, use a wrist cushion at the computer, create an ergonomic work station, wear wrist braces, stretch, and schedule another massage.

Joe meets me at the front desk after the session. "I have less pain and numbness in my arm. The burning and tingling are gone."

"Are you going to keep the arm?"

"I'll wait and see. If it's still attached in a week, I promise to keep the appointment I'm about to make.

HER REVENGE

BY YOKO NAGMUNE REESE

My cat
slips into view
as I type a poem.
Her head nudges my cheek
snuggles up to my arm
presses my hand.

Frustrated by no response
she steps on the keyboard
with all four paws
walks across
turns around
passes through, tickling
my nose with her fluffy long tail.

An indecipherable new poem
on the screen.

WRITING FOR MAGAZINES – A CLASS REVIEW

BY CHAR TIERNEY

The Internet has opened a new world with broadening horizons. Melody Groves uses her experience with writing for magazines to teach how simple it can be to start having your own works published in the approximately 9000 magazines available online and in hard copy. Her informative and motivating two-session class, "Writing for Magazines" covered aspects of the field such as; how to find an appropriate topic for articles, where to send query letters, selling the same story to other markets, and the ins and outs of a strong four-paragraph query letter.

Material provided in the class showed how to locate and examine the magazine's Masthead, where you find the various editors of the magazine. Picking the appropriate editor for your submission is an important element in the query process.

Melody emphasized an article is not written before a query letter goes out. The query letter presents the idea for the article, and the accepting editor decides the angle they want on the story, the length of the article, and whether they want photos. You save wasted time by not writing your piece until you receive a response and understand the editor's wishes. Once a reply is received with a word count request, keep to that number very closely, even to the exact number, if possible.

Reading the magazine to which you want to submit an article, gives insights about how to frame your own piece.

- What length are their usual stories?
- What is the tone/mood/style of the magazine?
- What is the education level of their readers?
- Do they use long words or short words, and do they adhere to APA Style, or to Chicago style, or another?
- What sources do they use and what is the caliber of their experts?
- What quotes and statistics do they use and where are they inserted in the magazine's stories?

All these details provide the information needed to take an informed approach to your own article.

A well written, four-paragraph query letter may be all it takes to get your article or story sold. Paragraph one should start with a hook; something sharp to catch the interest of the very busy editor. You might include a quote or statistic in this portion of the query.

The second paragraph reveals what your thoughts are on the article. Now that you have hooked them to your idea, what do they need to briefly know about the topic? This paragraph is also where you can make statements revealing that you are familiar with their magazine and explain briefly why your story fits in so well.

The third paragraph might show your expertise in the field, or writing experience, or where you have been previously published.

The fourth paragraph is a good place to inform the editor when you have photos available, and to tell them that you look forward to working with them. Don't forget to end with a friendly good-bye, such as Cheers, or Best wishes.

Once you receive a favorable response, write the article using the style that you found in the magazine. Your hook or lead from your query letter should provide a strong start. Overall, a typical pattern is to make a statement, then support it. Make another statement, then support it, and so forth.

When I decided to take the class, I really could not imagine my work published in magazines. There was a hint of bravado in my signing up, then showing up at the SWW office for the first Saturday session. But, by the time I left the class, I was confident that I can indeed write for magazines.

SUBARUS ARE DELICIOUS!

BY PATRICIA WALKOW

"My dog ate my car."

"Excuse me?"

"My dog ate my car." Just five words. I pointed to the damage and noticed the service manager's raised eyebrows, wry smirk, and open mouth. Today was the third time in the past fourteen years I had to utter those five same exact words.

"Well, that's a first," I heard him say.

I'm apparently a slow learner about leaving dogs alone in cars.

The damage proved dogs really do like Subarus. Brand new, top-of-the-line Subaru. Last night my husband, Walter, and I went out to dinner, took the dog with us, and left him in the car. This routine is not new for Magic, a fifteen-month-old adolescent German Shepherd-Siberian Husky-mix rescue dog. He loves hanging out in the car as though it is his private, mobile dog house. And last night, he relished eating the knobs of my climate control system, proving he really does enjoy the car.

He destroyed the two knobs of the center dashboard's climate control panel. They turn the interior dials that set temperature.

These knobs are back-lit, so there is an electrical contact that transmits the temperature setting to the climate control system in order to permit each front-seat passenger to adjust the temperature on their side of the car. The dials work just fine. But I can't tell if I am setting the temperature to 62 or 82 degrees until I am either freezing or roasting. Since they are lit, it looks like two bright white eyeballs are staring at me all the time.

In genuine planned-obsolescence fashion, you can't just purchase replacement knobs and get them installed. That would be un-American.

Instead, the entire climate control panel inserted into the dashboard needs to be replaced. What should be priced at $50 will cost almost $500. Just pull out the old unit—which, let me remind you—works just fine except for no knobs—plug in the new unit, and charge the customer $456.10. Oh, and be sure the customer has a chance to hear the mechanics at the dealer guffaw at your dog's bad behavior. Maybe submit it as an anecdote to *The Antics of Subaru-Loving Dogs*. Meanwhile, my dog looks at me with his big, soulful eyes, pants with his tongue sticking out an inch, and I kiss him on top of his head.

You missed me, Magic, is that it? It's not your fault, boy, even though I've left you in the car dozens of times and you never did anything like this!

I am now researching metal barriers between the front and back seats.

I should have known, though.

Previously, with another dog—Ranger—my husband dropped a dog biscuit between the driver's seat and center floor console in his brand-new Acura MDX. The dog found it three nights later. He had to struggle in his effort, and I am certain it took him at least a few minutes to shred the highly-adjustable and heated (meaning very expensive) leather seat to get at his doggie cookie. The car was a week old and it took six weeks for the color to return to my husband's face and the dealer to stop laughing.

But Ranger was an excellent traveler and usually quite reliable when left alone in a car.

But one day I forgot I had wrapped some bacon for him from a Denny's breakfast and left it overnight in the glove box of my Toyota Avalon. The following day I went out to breakfast again and the dog remained in the car that morning.

Have you ever seen a shredded glove box?

That little mishap required the dealer to keep the car for three days to remove the entire dashboard, replace the glove box, and reassemble everything. I still see the dealer's repair staff scratching their heads over that one.

Clearly, our dogs have made blithering idiots of Walter and me. Idiots who can't resist a dog's tilt of the head. Idiots who would probably pat the dog on the head as it munches on a $1,000 smart phone while we comment how cute he looks doing it.

But that hasn't happened yet.

We just buy TV remote controls by the three-pack and computer mouse multi-packs. We run through a checklist of what we need to hide before we leave the house without our dog. We've learned that anything that has our scent on it is fair game, despite two bins of mangled doggie chew toys.

So, we tolerate the felonies our dogs have committed. I try to understand why, since the damage has cost quite a bit of money, and I believe the answer is simple: We have been hopelessly in love with any dog we've owned. Secretly, I think my husband is proud of our dogs' misbehavior and we always absolve them of the mortal sins they commit in the dog-human universe.

But possibly, it is something more.

Reflecting on my lack of common sense when it comes to dogs and destruction, I realized that if we humans possessed the capacity to forgive people's transgressions as readily as our willingness to forgive our dogs' shortcomings, perhaps we would approach the nobility of the canine species.

On the other hand, maybe I should have accepted my friend's offer to use his gun. But I'd probably shoot myself in the foot, and then Magic would comfort me, crunch 9-1-1 on my phone to call emergency services, and lick my face while waiting for the paramedics to show up.

I'd then give him his own set of car keys, a remote control or two, and a brand-new ergonomic computer mouse.

A Subaru Dog Car   Photo by Rose Marie Kern

MY DEAD CATS

BY PATRICIA MOORMAN

Mikie was adopted after
My husband died of cancer.
Why? My husband joked
About reincarnating as a cat.
What better reason than that?
Mikie was my anchor
Until he also died of cancer.

Pumpkin had topaz eyes
And gold flecked fur.
Her spirit could not be confined,
She had to explore.
With a screech of brakes and scream
She died one night on the street.
I still hear that scream.

Vickie chose me at the shelter.
Her eyes demanded that I take her.
I brought her home, sick and lame.
Soon, she was strong again.
She grabbed the hearts of everyone.
When she died,
So many cried.

SAGE ADVICE

Articles by experts on topics related to writing have appeared every month in the Sage. They run the gamut from the writing process to editing, publishing and marketing. We start here with our monthly writing advice column—*Ask Chaucer*--and end with the best advice we can give: *Keep Writing*.

ASK CHAUCER

Dear Chaucer,
I've written a novel, but I'm told I don't have a hook. What does this mean?
New Writer

Dear New,

A hook is what draws the reader into a story or book. It must be compelling, and is best if it creates questions. For example: "Above his head, in the cold, dark, wind-creaked rafters of the tobacco barn, Charley Bandy sees withered souls." (from *The End of War* by David L. Robbins) This compelling first line leaves us wondering who Charley Bandy is and why he sees withered souls instead of tobacco leaves. It immediately draws us into the story.

One misstep often made by new writers is starting the story at the very beginning. "I was born on a log cabin" probably won't encourage an agent to read on. A good hook starts in the middle of the action and invites the reader to discover what's going on. The reader doesn't need or want to know everything there is to know about the characters up front. It is the act of discovery that delights us all.

Look at your work to see if you're sharing the character's backstory at the beginning. If so, take it out. Backstory is like salt and pepper; sprinkle just a little throughout the book where it is really needed and your reader will enjoy it more.

Remember, agents and editors read a lot of work. If your hook isn't in the first page or so, they probably won't read on.

Good luck hooking that editor!

Signed,
Chaucer

GOAL SETTING

BY FRED AIKEN

As I write this, it is the first week in January, which means it is time to formulate my personal and business goals for this year (2018). The system that I use is the **SMARTER** system, which stands for:

Specific, Measurable, Achievable, Realistic, Time- dependent, Evaluated, and Reformulated

- ☒ The goal must be specific, not general.
- ☒ The goal must be quantifiable, meaning that it can be measured.
- ☒ The goal must be achievable, given my time and resources and other things within the sphere of my control.
- ☒ The goal must be realistic, given my education/knowledge and resources (time and financial).
- ☒ The goal must be time dependent having a definite beginning and ending date.
- ☒ The goal must be evaluated periodically
- ☒ The goal must be reformulated, if necessary, to get the goal back on track to successful completion.

This year, I have reduced the number of goals to twenty-six: nine personal goals and seventeen writing goals. Each meets the SMARTER system criteria. The business goals for 2018 will be:

☒ Spend 1,500 hours on Writing Related Activities.

☒ Attend the Romance Writers of America national conference in Denver.

☒ Attend the Super Stars conference in Colorado Springs.

☒ Attend Bubonicon.

☒ Write a weekly Thoughts for Tuesday blog post and a biweekly Friday Food for Thought blog post for my website

☒ Write a semi-annual writer's newsletter to subscribers of my website.

☒ Read a minimum of five books per quarter, either genre or craft.

☒ Write one Devotional per quarter and submit it for publication.

☒ Take one workshop or class per quarter.

☒ Enter one writing contest per quarter.

☒ Participate in the 2018 NaNoWriMo event.

☒ Revive the Cosmic Connection SF Critique Group during the Calendar year.

☒ Present one workshop or class during 2018.

☒ Write and submit six articles for the SWW Sage this year.

☒ Update my Writer's Business Plan for 2018.

☒ Write two hundred fifty thousand new words, sixty two thousand one hundred seventy-five new words per quarter.

☒ Send out at least one short story per month to magazines and keep them in circulation until sold, and send out one novel this year and keep it in circulation until sold.

I have also prepared my accountability spreadsheet to record my progress in meeting these seventeen goals. At the end of each quarter, I will evaluate my progress in meeting these goals and adjust the next quarter goals accordingly so that I will stay on course to have met each goal by December 31, 2018.

For more information on the SMARTER Goal method and how I handled the quarterly goals, visit my website and while you are there, sign up for my newsletter!

WWW: The Writing and Thoughts of FredAAikenWriter.com/Thoughts for Tuesday.

AN AUTHOR'S GUIDE TO COMIC CONS

BY ZACHRY WHEELER

As an author, what if I told you that there are places in the world where your core audience gathers to listen to whatever you have to say, and then purchase your books? Seems like a pipe dream, I know. Perhaps an elaborate prank. But at the risk of sounding like a charismatic cult leader, yes, they *do* exist. And I can show you where they are. And for a small donation ...

In all seriousness, this isn't fantasy, but it would help if you write fantasy. Science fiction and fantasy writers have a remarkable tool available to them that they should be milking for all its worth. I'm talking, of course, about comic conventions.

What, kind sir, is a comic convention? Don't think about it too hard, it's just a place where geeks and nerds gather to indulge in geeky and nerdy things. There are celebrity guests, discussion panels, costume contests, and booths full of colorful merchandise. That last one is where you come in.

Most comic cons separate their merchandise booths into two sections: Vendors and Artist Alley. Vendors sell anything and everything related to geek culture; prints, toys, games, apparel, knickknacks, and yes, the occasional comic book. The Artist Alley is where artists sell their original works. As an author, you qualify, and here's the best part: the Artist Alley is simultaneously the most popular *and cheapest* area in the entire convention. Anyone can sell a Deadpool bobblehead, but not everyone can sell an original print of Deadpool playing with his own bobblehead.

This is why the Artist Alley is so powerful for authors. Your books qualify as original works, so you can join the army of artists selling their art. Promoters love the Artist Alley because comic fans love comic artists. The assumption is also made that artists, being artists, are struggling to pay their rent, so they offer the deepest discounts for booths, often *half* the price of vendor booths.

Which brings us to the million dollar question. How much are the booths? Rest assured, they are nowhere near a million dollars (unless you're attending the massive San Diego Comic Con, but that's a whole other can of nerds). Typically, booths range from $50 to $400, and that's for the entire weekend. You also get free passes to the con, your own table with chairs, and a cool vendor pass to distinguish you from the peons.

So why the big swing in prices? Well, some cons are more popular than others. If you want to sling your wares at the Roswell Galacticon, it will cost you about $50. But, if you're lucky enough to score a booth at the huge Denver or Phoenix cons, you're going to have to dig deeper into the wallet. Think of it like this: the bigger the crowd, the bigger the cost. But, do not let the price points rattle you. Fans attend cons with a burning desire to buy stuff. It's not like you're hocking books in the streets. With the right attitude and a good elevator pitch, you will almost certainly cover your expenses and score a sizeable profit.

As a simple example, I manned an Artist Alley booth at the Albuquerque Comic Con shortly after the release of my debut novel *Transient*. Booth prices were $200 for the entire weekend, a great value for the crowd size. I brought 80 copies of the book along with a bunch of promo freebies (very important, will discuss those shortly). I priced them at $10 each and sold 78 of them. That's $780, which more than covered the entire con and all printing costs. I wasn't even trying to make a profit. I just wanted to promote my works and, best case scenario, cover my booth costs. And without breaking a sweat, I left with a healthy profit.

Sounds like a barrel of fantastic awesomeness. So what's the catch, con man? Yes, there is a catch. A very, very, very big catch. And I already know that it will be a deal-breaker for many authors. You must, and I cannot stress this enough, be personable. I can hear the shrieks of hysteria coming from several of you, but this is non-negotiable. The single worst thing you can do as a booth jockey is be shy. You have a sea of target clientele walking by you at all times. If you're afraid to talk to them, then you have no business being there. I cannot tell you how many times I have walked by an artist booth, only to see them face down in their smartphone. For pity's sake, engage your audience.

Okay, so you've made peace with the necessary extroversion. Now what? Well, it's time to build a killer booth. Authors, more than anyone else, succumb to booth blandness. This is a *comic con*, an event full of pulsing colors, neon spandex, and scantily clad cosplayers. You *must* stand out. It's not enough to drop your books on a table with price tags. You need posters, promo cards, signage, freebies, whatever it takes to say "look at me, I'm a cool author with fun stories." One of my favorite things to do is dress up as a popular character from my genre. You'll hook potential readers as a fellow fan. I write science fiction, so on the busiest day of the con, I dress up as Jayne Cobb from Firefly. At one point, I sold three books after singing *The Hero of Canton* with a Serenity ensemble.

Oh, and the cons usually sell beer, so that helps.

A few notes on freebies: they can be literally anything related to you and your work. I always have a ton of business cards spread out on the table with book covers on one side and my author info on the other. Pro tip: don't overdo the personal details. Your name, website, and social media handles are more than enough. I get all my cards and posters from VistaPrint, an easy and affordable online option. Get creative. I used to be in rock bands once upon a time, so I always bring a stack of old CDs to give away.

Comic cons can be insanely rewarding (and highly profitable) if you play them right, but you have to be smart about it. Some other things to consider:

- You *must* be able to take credit cards. You live in a digital world, so leverage it. If you manage to hook a reader, but can't take their preferred method of payment, then you should slap yourself and go hide under a rock. I use Square, an easy option that allows you to swipe cards on your smartphone.

- Power is also an issue because you want your phone up at all times for transactions and promo pics. I always bring a portable USB charger, which you can nab on Amazon for cheap.

- Polish and exploit your social media presence. You should announce your events and booth locations as they approach. And, be sure to post *during* the event (that means having all your apps connected and up to date). One of my favorite instances was when Ming Chen of AMC's Comic Book Men snatched a copy of *Transient*. He posed for a pic and I blasted it through Facebook, Twitter, and Instagram before he even got back to his booth. That's right, celebrity endorsements! You never know what will happen, so be prepared for it.

How much should I price my books?

Whatever you do, don't get greedy. Always remember that the primary reason you are there is to *market*, not sell. If I don't sell a single book, but give out 100 business cards, I still consider that a successful convention.

That being said, $10 is my magic number. Plus, whole numbers attract impulse buys. At that price point, I usually manage to cover booth and printing costs. In short, use good judgement. If you're selling a 120K-word tome, then you can probably ask for $20. But, if you're selling a 60K-word YA novel, asking $20 will destroy your sales potential.

Pro tip: include sales tax in a whole price. Extra dollars and cents just serve to annoy your customers.

Wow, there are a ton of conventions. Which one should I choose?

Start small and work your way up. If you've never done a con before, don't tackle the big ones because you need to hone an expectation. Try a small local event first. You need to figure out what works and what doesn't. And if you've never been to a con, I recommend attending a few as a fan before manning a booth. Get a feel for how vendors interact with customers. Take notes, snap pics, have fun.

Engaging people is hard for me. How can I get over it?

Fear not. These are comic cons, basically a giant mob of socially awkward fanboys. You're not giving a speech at Harvard, so don't let it intimidate you. You're among friends who *want* to talk about the same stuff you do. That's the whole point of being there. But, it's up to *you* to initiate that conversation. Once you get the hang of it, it becomes second nature. Plus, there's a lot of camaraderie among vendors. They'll make you feel right at home (and give you pro tips).

What if I need to change something mid-convention?

You will, so plan for it. You'll be amazed by all the tiny little details that you never think to consider. As a simple example, I have hanging banners that flank my booth. But at one con, my booth was directly below an AC vent. The posters swayed back and forth on the stands, so I needed to secure them. Luckily, I had brought some tape. I always bring a small tackle box full of pins, clips, tape, adapters, etc. It's an old habit I picked up from performing in rock bands. Do not assume that the con will provide.

Also, do not rely on a single pitch. Your audience will change throughout the con. The early hours are typically family-friendly, while the evening hours are much more saucy. You have to mold to the environment. For example, I keep a folder full of different signage options, which allows me to cater to the current audience. I don't hang the signs themselves, I use acrylic stands and swap out as needed.

I tried a con booth and barely sold anything. What gives?

Cons are hit and miss by nature and not all of them will be profitable. A myriad of factors go into making a con *financially* successful. But, that's not the point. Remember that you're there to promote yourself first and foremost. Did you engage your audience? Did you build contacts? Did you give away a bunch of cards and freebies? If the answer is no, then the con is not to blame. Time to re-evaluate your approach.

I can't afford booths at big cons. What are my options?

It's not uncommon for authors to share booths in order to cut costs. This is especially true for writers groups. When the big cons roll around, a few of my author friends may get together to share the expense, which can add up quick when you throw in hotels, travel, etc. Sometimes the organization itself will share the cost in order to gain exposure. Plus, it's always nice to have friends there to alleviate the mental stress (and cover bathroom breaks). Sure, your space is smaller and it might affect your sales a bit, but you gain access to the most valuable part: a massive sea of target readers.

BLOGGING YOUR WAY TO SUCCESS

BY ROB SPIEGEL, SWW VP

Why Start a Blog?

A blog can be a powerful tool to create, build, and hold a reading audience. Whatever your interest, you can build a blog around it: genre fiction, poetry, business knowhow, gardening, caregiving. One of my blogging students created an award-winning blog about caring for an ailing spouse. The goal of that blog was simple honesty about everything that's involved in home-based spousal care.

I've been writing blogs for 20 years. I began back when they were called "web logs." I turned a self-syndicated business column into a blog simply by sending the column to websites. The idea fit, since the informal blogging language matches the conversational tone of a column. The newspaper column is indeed the antecedent for the blog.

Here are some of the reasons for launching a blog:

Blogging doesn't cost anything. Blogging tools have become amazingly user friendly, and they're free if you don't add fancy features such as the ability to sell goods. WordPress is the grand supermarket of blogs, with millions of bloggers aboard. Other free blogging platforms include Blogger, Medium, and Tumblr. You can find plenty of others, but these four are known for their powerful communities and ease of use.

I launched my personal blog on WordPress. Within 45 minutes of learning the system, I had my first blog go live. Within eight months, I had more than 2,500 visitors and 5,000 page views. I spent a bit of time each day reaching out to grab readers, and I posted three times per week. Not a huge amount of work.

You get practice writing on a regular schedule. Nothing improves your writing skills like writing. A blog is a commitment to a schedule to produce work that you're willing to share with the world. Once you get on a regular schedule, you'll see improvements in your ability to connect with readers. Comments from those readers will let you know when you're connecting and when you're not. It's a wonderful feedback loop.

You can test out writing ideas. Blogging gets fun when you start taking changes with your writing. I went through one period when I tried to write spirituality posts in prose poetry form. I'm still not sure the attempt was a success, but it did prompt interesting comments from readers. The ability to stretch your own writing limits may be the most valuable aspect of blogging. Where else can you try out new writing wings in front of regular readers?

You can build an audience for a book. My primary goal in starting a spirituality blog was to attract sufficient readers to bolster my pitch to do a book the subject. Publishers and agents love it when you have built-in readers. The posts themselves – I did about 200 – can become the source material for your book. The experiment worked. A found an appropriate agent who was interested in seeing my book proposal.

You can promote your books. I launched my first blog – an offshoot of my newspaper column – for the express purpose of promoting my books. I was promoting five books I had written on various aspects of home-business and internet enterprise. I needed to reach potential book buyers. So, I wrote a column for the late-great *Albuquerque Tribune*, and used the column as a blog that I sold or gave away to a few dozen entrepreneurial websites. At the end of each column was a blurb promoting one of my books. I did that for six years – that's a lot of readers looking at the blurb over many, many, many weeks. That's a form self-promotion I got paid to write.

You can promote a business. If you run a business, a blog can work wonderfully as a promotion tool. Major companies such as Google, Microsoft, and Facebook regularly blog to keep their communities in the loop about new features and products. Consultants – from therapists to yoga teachers – use blogs to teach their client communities. Many authors set up their blogs to accept PayPal and credit cards to sell their books directly from their blog sites.

While there are a ton of ways to promote a business through a blog, the essential value of a blog is the ability to connect with readers who have a deep interest in your subject. Through that connectivity, you can communicate the benefits of your services or products. And you can build credibility simply by sharing your knowledge.

Beyond all those reasons, you get to connect with people all over the globe. Some of my dearest readers were scattered in faraway places such as Sweden, Australia, and India. All we had in common was an interest in the subject and the shared ability to read and write in English. It's like having thousands of pen pals.

How to Build an Audience for Your Blog

In part one of this two-part article, we looked at the reasons to launch a blog – how it helps your writing career. While the practice of writing blogs is inherently valuable – all writing teaches you how to write – the true goal of blogging is to create a reading audience.

Here are 15 tactics you can use to build a reading audience. I've tried every one, and each one contributes to growing your readership. To succeed in driving an audience that continually grows, you have to do most – if not all – of these efforts. Some are simply a matter of focusing your writing. Others take a commitment of time.

Create content with a known audience in mind. Whether you blog about fly fishing, needlepoint, or growing peppers, pick a subject that matches your passion, one that has plenty of readers actively seeking information or shared experience.

Participate in communities where potential readers already gather. Creating a reading community from scratch is time-consuming and may ultimately prove fruitless. Choose a subject for your blog that already has an existing community of bloggers and websites. Visit those, read those blogs, and interact with your fellow enthusiasts.

Use social media to share your posts. Not everyone you know will be aware that you're writing a blog, but they might check out your blog if you post it on Facebook or Twitter. Blogging platforms make it easy to share posts on social media. It's just a matter of indicating on your blogging platform what social media to share your posts on. Once you've set it up, your posts will appear automatically on your social media. I received a huge bump in readers when a friend of mine started sharing my posts on his Facebook page – he had 3,000 friends.

Pay attention to your metrics and analytics. Make your blog more reader friendly by paying attention to what your readers like and what they don't care for. What posts are getting the most likes and comments? What posts are getting re-blogged? Pay attention to your metrics and you'll see patterns that will help you create posts that get attention.

Add graphics to each post. Readers want to see something besides words. Use some imagination to match images with your writing. When you find an image, make sure you give credit to the source of the image.

Reference your own posts and the posts of others. If you cover a subject in depth, you'll find that it's handy to include links to earlier posts. This is not only helpful to your reader, it also gets your reader more deeply involved in your blog. Include links to related posts by other bloggers and you'll further expand your network.

Guest posts and re-blogs. You can ask fellow bloggers to write a guest post on your blog. Plus, most blogging platforms make it easy to re-blog a post on your subject. My readership started to increase noticeably when other bloggers started to re-blog some of my posts.

Commit to a posting frequency. Posting once every couple weeks is not sufficient if you want to build a readership. I started out posting once a week. That didn't seem to be quite enough, so I shifted to twice a week. Once ratcheted up to three times a week, it was easier to build readership. That doesn't mean you need to write a full post each time. You can re-blog posts from other writers, or you can write a couple of sentences pointing to a cool site or blog you found.

Interact with other bloggers by liking, following, and commenting. One of the surest ways to create a community or readers is to read and comment on related blogs. There are three ways you can interact with fellow bloggers: by liking their posts, by "following" or subscribing to their blog, and by commenting on individual posts. Once you begin to like, follow, and comment on other blogs, they'll start to like, follow, and comment on your blog.

Put your blogging address in your email signature. Add a link to your blog in your email signature. You'll get clicks. People are curious. A certain percentage of those clickers will become regular readers.

Make sure your blog address appears every time you comment online. When commenting on the blogs of others, include your blog link. Blogging platforms do this automatically, but that doesn't happen if you comment on an article on a website. So include your blog link manually with your comments.

Put your blog address in your profiles and content. Every time you write a profile for yourself, every time you write an article, make sure you end with a blurb about your blog that includes a link.

Make a list of post ideas. Avoid the dreary problem of "what am I going to write about today?" I made a list of 20 post ideas. Every time I use one of the ideas, I add a new one. That way I am never stumped for a topic. That also means I'm never using my weakest idea.

Aggregate the best blogs and best posts with a best-of in your niche. One simple and effective post – especially when you've run out of cool ideas – is to post a list of great posts on your subject. Readers love "best-of" link collections.

Don't give up. In the words of Winston Churchill, "Never, never, never, never give up." Most bloggers give up before their readership has a chance to grow. It takes time. In the first three or four months, my readership grew slowly. I would get a few dozen readers at best. A year later, hundreds of readers were clicking on each post.

NICHE MARKETS

BY ROSE MARIE KERN

If you are reading this article than you are probably a member of SouthWest Writers--which means you love to write. You may have written a couple hundred short stories before you even began looking at the possibility of publishing.

Many people want to write stories for themselves and pray that publishers will see how brilliant they are. Others realize that they must write with a specific audience in mind in order for their work to be accepted. That's where this article is leading.

You would really love it if your writing produced an income. You could wait upon the big publishing houses to flock to your door with offers, or you could be more proactive and investigate how best to use your talents. You could find one or more niches that need your talents and exploit them.

A **niche** is a focused, targetable part of the market. You are a specialist providing a product or service that focuses on specific client group's needs, which cannot, or are not, addressed by mainstream providers.

Niche writing requires that you have some expertise in one or more areas. Most niche writing does not start with book publishing--it starts with submitting articles or stories to magazines, either printed or online. You build an audience and eventually you put out a book.

NOTICE I said YOU put out a book. Again, you are the one who needs to be proactive. You can write books all day long, you could self-publish, but you need to have a following, a marketing scheme, and a method of distribution. To do this, you must find a niche.

Everyone has something they can write about that others care about. Here at SWW we have several successful authors whose niches have earned them national attention.

Gail Ruben, the *Doyenne of Death*, writes for funeral magazines and has two books on the market. She is invited to speak for funeral directors' conferences.

Dr. Susan Cooper writes knowledgably (and amusingly) about a topic that disgusts most people: mold. She also found a second niche market and wrote a book titled "Football Facts for Females."

A friend of mine loves to quilt. Patsy has quilted all kinds of lovely designs and participated in quilting clubs. She noticed that she and all the others in the group had one complaint. When they were done creating the beautiful fronts of the quilts, they had to do the quilting that holds the layers together, which took a long time and was tedious.

Patsy discovered that she could make a lot of money by doing the quilting. She creates beautiful designs for backings which complement the fronts. She created beautiful quilting designs that complement the front, and has a special "long-arm" sewing machine that can be programed to stitch those designs. She writes about that process.

I have written three books and hundreds of articles on diverse topics: Aviation, Fundraising Events and Solar Cooking. The two that are true niches--aviation and solar cooking--have done very well. It turned out that Fundraising is more widely written about and did only marginally well.

In 2001 I saw a friend use a solar cooker and I just had to buy one. I searched everywhere for ideas and instructions on cooking family-sized meals and found none, except for those printed in the small pamphlet that came with my solar cooker.

Over the next year I did a lot of experimenting with meats, vegetables, casseroles, desserts, appetizers and anything else I could think of. I spoke to others who had solar cookers and got their favorite recipes. I wrote an article on solar cooking for *Solar Today* Magazine and one for *Countryside* Magazine. Then in 2003 I put it all together into "*The Solar Chef--a Southwestern Recipe Book for Solar Cooking.*" This book is now in its 8th edition and still sells a few hundred copies a year.

My first day at a SouthWest Writers' meeting I introduced myself and told people that I was an air traffic control specialist. Jack Hickman, the editor of a local pilot club's newsletter, asked me to write an article for him. That article was quickly picked up and reprinted by other pilot groups. The editor of a national aviation magazine read it and asked if they could publish it. Then he called and asked for more. I've had over 400 articles published on the subjects of Air Traffic Control and Aviation Weather.

My most recent book, *Air to Ground*, is a guide written for pilots about air traffic control. After a decade of writing for magazines I had built a fan base and my magazine editors have promoted me widely.

Here are a few questions you need to ask yourself:
- So, where does your audience hang out?
- Where, when and what do they buy?
- Are you an expert at something?
- Do you have insights and ideas on topics that interest a number of others?
- Can you identify a need?

Below is a diagram with different blocks where you can write in information on your careers, jobs, avocations, hobbies, places you've traveled, places you've lived, experiences you can't forget, talents you recognize in yourself, passions, and "other" things that defy categories.

As you can see I have listed my own for you--the trick is to use the list to find how all these types of things can cross over and potentially find niches you are particularly well suited to write about.   The yellow block in the center lists the areas of crossover I have identified and exploited.

Discovering more about yourself expands your opportunities for publication - try it for yourself!

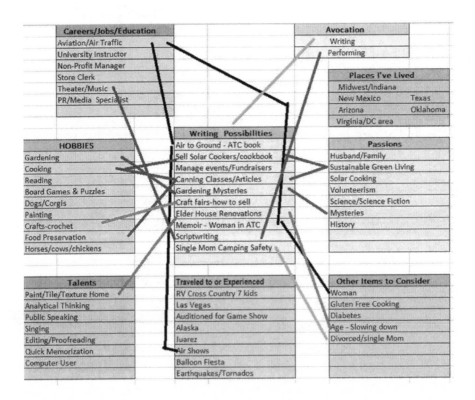

Careers/Jobs/Education	
Aviation/Air Traffic	
University Instructor	
Non-Profit Manager	
Store Clerk	
Theater/Music	
PR/Media Specialist	

Avocation	
Writing	
Performing	

Places I've Lived	
Midwest/Indiana	
New Mexico	Texas
Arizona	Oklahoma
Virginia/DC area	

HOBBIES
Gardening
Cooking
Reading
Board Games & Puzzles
Dogs/Corgis
Painting
Crafts-crochet
Food Preservation
Horses/cows/chickens

Writing Possibilities
Air to Ground - ATC book
Sell Solar Cookers/cookbook
Manage events/Fundraisers
Canning Classes/Articles
Gardening Mysteries
Craft fairs-how to sell
Elder House Renovations
Memoir - Woman in ATC
Scriptwriting
Single Mom Camping Safety

Passions
Husband/Family
Sustainable Green Living
Solar Cooking
Volunteerism
Science/Science Fiction
Mysteries
History

Talents
Paint/Tile/Texture Home
Analytical Thinking
Public Speaking
Singing
Editing/Proofreading
Quick Memorization
Computer User

Traveled to or Experienced
RV Cross Country 7 kids
Las Vegas
Auditioned for Game Show
Alaska
Juarez
Air Shows
Balloon Fiesta
Earthquakes/Tornados

Other Items to Consider
Woman
Gluten Free Cooking
Diabetes
Age - Slowing down
Divorced/single Mom

SUSPENSE BUILDERS

BY KIRT HICKMAN

For many writers, the challenge of story lies in how to plot, rather than plod, through the long, languid, middle of the novel. The key to holding your reader's attention lies in the art of maintaining suspense. This article presents a list of elements that will increase the suspense in your story. Build as many into your plot as it can accommodate.

Make at least one character especially violent or adversarial:

This character is a wild card. He should have the ability and inclination to severely and unexpectedly hurt your hero (or at least hurt your hero's chances of achieving her goal).

Spring surprises:

Keep the reader guessing. Provide many obstacles that come at your hero when she least expects them and when your reader least expects them. Provide at least one surprise turning point in each chapter. These surprises must not be contrived events, however. They must stem from the characters, their goals, and their motivations.

Mislead your reader:

If you mislead your reader, the surprises will have more impact. Nevertheless, you must play fair. Leave clues that are consistent with who your characters are—even if the characters are different than your reader believes them to be.

Do your worst:

In every scene, ask yourself: What's the worst thing that could happen to the hero? Then make it happen.

Take away that which is most important to your hero:

What does your hero care about more than anything else? Take it away, or better yet, destroy it. At the very least, put it at risk.

Haunt your hero with memories of a past failure:

Relate the failure to the events in the book. Put your hero in the same situation she was in when she experienced her failure. Use her memories of that failure to undermine her confidence and make her challenges more difficult and more personal.

Turn the environment loose upon your characters:

In my science fiction novel, *Worlds Asunder*, the vacuum of space lurks beyond the walls of the buildings, vehicles, and pressure suits that keep my characters alive. I frequently turn it loose inside.

For the purpose of building suspense, "environment" doesn't have to mean "natural phenomena." It can refer to any element of the character's surroundings that is beyond the control of the main characters, including sociological, political, or economic circumstances and events. To keep an environmental event from seeming contrived, establish early that such an event is possible.

Employ phobias:

What is your hero afraid of? Make him confront the source of his fear. If you choose something the reader also fears, it will heighten his emotional response.

Never make anything easy:

Turn all your minor challenges into major ordeals. Make even simple tasks difficult if circumstances can justify your doing so.

Show that the danger is real:

Hurt your hero, kill a good guy, or both. If you kill someone your hero cares about, it will raise the personal stakes and inject a strong emotional element into your plot. At one point in *Worlds Asunder*, my hero is hospitalized for his wounds following a battle for his life. In addition, several good guys die, including one of my hero's closest relatives. This shows that the threat to him is very real.

Impose a deadline:

This is the ticking clock. It need not be a clock the hero can see, or one with a specified time to zero, but one way or another you must create a sense of urgency.

In *Worlds Asunder*, the political events surrounding my hero's investigation escalate toward war. If he can solve the case in time, his findings might diffuse the building crisis. He doesn't know how much time he has, but he and the reader can see the escalation. In alternating scenes, the hero takes a step toward solving the case, and then political events expand. This creates an unseen clock. My hero and the reader are never quite sure it hasn't already reached zero, the point beyond which no one can stop the war.

Prevent your hero from running away:

You don't need to impose a physical barrier, but make your hero's need to stay in the conflict stronger than his desire to escape it. The same must be true for your villain. In *Worlds Asunder*, my hero wants to retire and go home to his family—that would be his escape—but averting war is much more important. He won't quit, even when the stakes rise and he must risk losing his own daughter.

Use these techniques in combination. Don't restrict yourself to one suspense builder per scene. Stack these elements one upon another, particularly in key scenes. This will compel your reader to keep turning the pages.

THE INDEPENDENT, FULL-SERVICE PUBLISHER

BY MARTY GERBER, PUBLISHER

It is a truism of the modern book world that self-publishing has made it easier than ever for an author to physically turn a manuscript into a book—and harder than ever to connect that book with readers.

For independent, full-service publishers like Terra Nova Books, this is the reality that has enabled us to thrive. In 2018, we have found, authors are realizing the value in many publishing areas of skills and knowledge that may be beyond their own, as well as the benefits of national distribution and marketing that make their work more than just one more title among the many millions on Amazon.

What we provide as a publisher is simple—everything! There is no way to scrimp and cut corners and still hope to find readers when faced with the almost-unbelievable competition of *800 books* being published in the U.S. *every day.*

Most of this deluge consists of books whose lack of professionalism is pretty easy for readers to spot. It jumps from the page, so to speak, when compared with titles from a quality-focused publishing house—a difference we make clear through the entire range of Terra Nova's complete package of services:

Editing, proofreading, layout, cover design, formatting for print and e-book, publication online and in paper- or hard-back, national distribution through a sales force calling on every bookstore in the country, and marketing via print and broadcast reviews/articles/interviews; author appearances; and the social media (as well as providing the "technical" essentials of ISBN, copyright, barcode, etc).

Terra Nova is always looking for worthwhile manuscripts in any genre. Our criteria are four:

- Is this book about something people will care to read?
- Does it not duplicate 10 or 12 (or maybe even 3 or 4) other books already out on the market?
- What's the writing like? Is it of professional quality, or can it be brought to that level through our editing process?
- Will the author truly commit to being our full partner in marketing this book?

Seems simple. But the major percentage of manuscripts submitted to us fall short. We ask for a synopsis of the book, chapter summaries, and two sample chapters (including the first), along with a cover letter outlining the intended audience for the work, the marketing the author believes will reach this audience most effectively, and the author's own planned role in these efforts—plus a short resume of the author's publishing, personal, and professional history.

Sometimes writers are put off by this. They have a wonderful book, they believe; it should be enough. So they turn to self-publishing—which is not necessarily a bad decision when made realistically. The problems come for those who don't truly understand what they're getting into, and what they're not.

"Self-publishing," of course, is almost always a misnomer. Very few are the writers who can—or want to—take all the many steps in the publishing process themselves. Thus, the typical self-publisher generally ends up:

- Taking a chance and hiring contractors whose skills are sometimes sadly deficient;
- Making decisions that he or she doesn't really have the background for; or
- Trusting to one of the online "packagers" like Lulu or CreateSpace—which often have serious drawbacks as well.

In addition, the author who goes this route usually finds there are virtually no bookstores anywhere that will carry the works of self-publishers—simply because retailers would rather do business with the industry's established distributors than with individual authors.

Undeniably, most books are sold on Amazon these days. Among those 800 published every day, there are many authors for whom what it offers is enough, and is the right way to go. But many others, I see increasingly, don't become clear on all the upsides and downsides until it's too late. There are few options left—maybe none—for authors with a good book that they can't get to the right readers, or for those with a less-good book after they realize it could have been better had they not tried to do so much themselves.

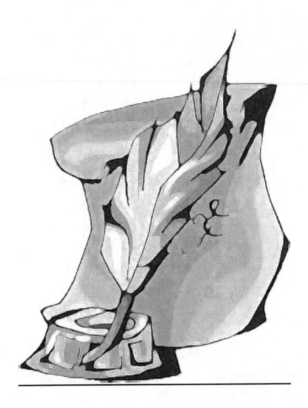

KEEP WRITING

BY SHERRI BURR

Super Bowl LI (51) belongs to history, but its lessons can teach in perpetuity. When the New England Patriots were down 0-0 in the first quarter, 3-21 in the second and 9-28 at the close of the third, it appeared the Atlanta Falcons had won their first National Football League Championship. But then something interesting happened in the fourth quarter. The Falcons started to play not to lose, and the Patriots played as if they had nothing to lose. After the game wrapped up with a Patriot victory in overtime, New England's coach was asked how his team turned it around. His response was, "We just kept competing.

For those of us engaged in the writing life, we must "keep writing." When a rejection letter arrives by snail mail, keep writing. When email queries are greeted with "Your work doesn't fit my list," keep writing. When your agent shops your book only to have editors respond, "The proposal feels half-baked," keep writing.

Writers must develop dreams as defined as a football goal line. In the fourth quarter, it seemed quarterback Tom Brady must have told his team, "We're headed to the goal line, we're going to score a touchdown, and then we're going to score two extra points." He must have stated clearly defined goals over and over again because the Patriots racked up score after score. They kept competing, and we must keep writing.

Ultimately, the only person who can stop you from fulfilling your writing goals is you. Toss your computer out the window or throw away all your paper and pencils in frustration, and you assure that your thoughts will not be recorded in physical form. Fail to appear in your office or designated writing space, and you guarantee nothing will be written. Never send anything out, and you certify nothing will be published.

Writers control their destinies. To stop producing is to stop challenging yourself. No matter how dire the straits might look, abandoning the course guarantees failure.

Athletes are schooled to develop selective memory, a trait that distinguishes champions from also-rans. Successful golfers may hit a stray shot, but they concentrate on the next one. Tennis players may watch opponents lob balls over their heads for winners, but they let go of their lost point. They breathe into missed opportunities and prepare for their next shots. So must writers.

When a query email receives a rejection, send out another one immediately. By focusing on the goal, you have less time to mourn a negative outcome. As the minutes ticked away into Super Bowl 51's overtime, the New England Patriots focused on their immediate challenge, to put the ball in the end zone one last time.

Successful athletes are known to develop tunnel vision toward their goals, and so must writers. If you dream of publishing a particular article or book, explore ways it can be rendered in physical form. Options abound from newsletters and magazines to blogs and newspapers.

Publishers seek books. Do you want a top New York publisher

to present your work to a wide audience? Would a regional or specialty press be better able to target your words to the intended market? Do you want to self-publish and completely control the distribution of your work and the accumulation of royalties? These are questions you should ask yourself based on your goals. Then determine how to fulfill your desires.

Just as athletes seeking to win must keep competing, so must writers. If success does come your way, start working on your next project. Do not replicate the Atlanta Falcons' strategy of playing "not to lose." They became complacent when they led their opponents by 25 points. "If we can just run out the clock, we will be champions," their body language conveyed. What happened? The clock expired and they were tied. Another fifteen minutes was added to the overtime clock, and the Falcons lost the coin toss, which permitted the New England Patriots to start. Eight plays later, the Patriots were in the end zone and confetti draped the stadium. Playing not to lose is setting up *to* lose.

No matter how well your last article or book was received, do not be content with your last advance or award. Another goal awaits completion. Keep writing.

SAGE AUTHORS' INFORMATION

All the authors featured in the Sage Anthology are members of the SouthWest Writers association. If the one you are looking for is not listed, it is because some of them preferred not to include a biography.

* * * * *

Goal Setting by Fred Aiken

Fred Aiken has been a member of SWW since 1996 and has served on the SWW board. He is an award winning professional writer, appearing in such magazines as Guideposts and Angels-on-Earth. He has been active in several other writing groups, such as LERA chapter of RWA, Croak and Dagger chapter of sisters in Crime, Writers to Writers. He is a retired educator, has written articles for the SWW Sage and has taught classes a number of times for SWW.

Mystery of the Dead Sisters by Lynn Andrepont

Lynn Andrepont holds a Master's Degree in English from the University of Southwestern Louisiana (now the University of Louisiana at Lafayette) and has enjoyed a long and successful career as a teacher, marketer, communicator, writer, and editor. She's written award-winning business publications and articles and several one-act plays—one of which was performed at the Quaigh Theater in New York City. She hopes her finished first novel, *Escape from Moon Village*, finds its way into publication soon. It's about a flourishing community that mysteriously disappeared 3,000 years ago at the archaeological site today known as Poverty Point in northern Louisiana.

Massage for Carpal Tunnel Syndrome by Jennifer Black

I'm a licensed massage therapist and have been a body worker since 2005.   Even though I'm still a registered massage therapy instructor, I gave up teaching to have more time to write. My husband and I live west of Rio Rancho, taking care of chickens, dogs, horses, and a cat.

Steel Town Girl by Dr. Irene Blea

Dr. Irene Blea is a New Mexico native with a Ph.D. in Sociology. She is the author of 7 academic textbooks, over 30 academic articles, 4 poetry chapbooks, and 4 novels. She was selected Best of Albuquerque in 2015 and again in 2018. Blea also is an award winning poet with a long tradition of writing feminist poetry. In 1987 she was awarded the Martin Luther King Jr. Literary Award in Denver, Colorado, and shared the stage with Allen Ginsberg and Andy Clausen. Blea writes daily, maintains a strong online presence via a blog, Facebook, and is a featured speaker at conferences, universities, and annual meetings. When she is not writing she is tending her flower garden.

Birds on a Wire by Dr. Joanne S. Bodin

Joanne is an award-winning author and poet. Her book of poetry, ***Piggybacked***, was a *finalist* in the New Mexico Book Awards. Her novel, ***Walking Fish***, won the New Mexico Book Award and the International Book Award in LGBT fiction. Her novel, ***Orchid of the Night,*** was a *finalist* in the 2018 Eric Hoffer Book Awards, *won second place* in the New Mexico Press Women 2018 Communication Contest, *won distinguished favorite* in the 2017 NYC Big Book Awards, and was a *winner* in the 2017 New Mexico/Arizona Book Awards in LGBT fiction. She is past vice president of the New Mexico State Poetry Society and is on the boards of Southwest Writers and the New Mexico Orchid Guild. Her poetry has appeared in numerous poetry anthologies.

Purple by Jay Brooks

I am a psychologist by profession, but my avocation is reading and writing. Reading has enriched and enlivened my life. I read everything including newspapers blown into my yard. I aspire to writing novels but currently enjoy short stories and verse. I find writing and writers endlessly fascinating.

Harping: Cheaper than Therapy
by Dr. Michele Lang Buchanan

Growing up inside the secretive "Manhattan Project", Michele went on to earn a Ph.D. and a long career in Special Education, teaching mostly Behavior Disordered children. Children do commit murder! After retiring, her love of the harp gestated for twenty years and bore her first novel, "Scota's Harp." Music entwined with Celtic history led her to facilitate the Celtic Singers of New Mexico, as well as a local harp circle of others in a love affair with strings. Her costume company, "Vestments," clothed many a SCA enthusiast, and she comes in costume to play at Renaissance Faires and Celtic Festivals. Children are now grown and gone, so she and her husband make their home in Albuquerque where he puts up with her social activism and extensive oil lamp collection. She is still looking for the genie!

Keep Writing by Dr. Sherri Burr

Sherri Burr is the Regents Professor and Dickason Chair Emerita at the University Of New Mexico School Of Law, where she joined the faculty in 1988 after having received degrees from Mount Holyoke College, Princeton University, and the Yale Law School. An internationally renowned lecturer, Burr has spoken at universities in Barbados, Canada, Chile, France, Greece, Japan, Mexico, Spain, and South Africa. She is the recipient of over a dozen awards for her writing, speeches and television show ARTS TALK, which she produced and hosted for 19 years. Burr has published 26 books, including the award-winning 2014 "A Short & Happy Guide to Financial Well-being."

Awakening by Yvonne Williams Casaus

Yvonne Williams Casaus is a Mom, Wife, Author, Speaker, Counselor, and Play Therapist. With a degree in Mechanical Engineering, she has been a Satellite Engineer, a Mission Planner, and has even worked for NASA. As an Author, she was spiritually inspired to share from her knowledge as a Therapist and Suicide Loss Survivor to help others find encouragement and inspiration through loss. She is currently the owner of Cottonwood Counseling, LLC where she specializes in treating trauma, PTSD, depression and anxiety. She is an independently licensed Clinical Mental Health Counselor (LPCC) and a Registered Play Therapist (RPT). She has been helping adults, children, adolescents, and families for over 13 years.

An Unusual Suitor by Brenda Cole

Brenda comes from a long line of story tellers, but she's the first one to put the stories on paper. "I entered my first writing contest at age 12 and have been writing ever since. Most of my published works are academic-Ecology, Archaeology and Biology along with poetry and short stories. My background is in Life Sciences and Speech and Theater. When I'm not teaching, editing or running seminars I'm doing something creative. My artistic outlets are painting, embroidery, knitting or watching and reading old-school Sci-Fi and Horror.

Bodrum by Patricia Conoway

I grew up in Pittsburgh, PA within walking distance to downtown. By age ten, I knew I'd leave Pittsburgh as soon as I could, and planned my escape. I got my degree in Psychology, was a cocktail waitress in New Orleans before, during, and after Mardi Gras, saved my tips and left for Europe within a year of graduation. I had to see and experience things other than the small townish, Irish Catholic and Italian neighbourhood I grew up in. I lived in Rome for over 8 months as an au pair, fell in love with an Italian, left, got an MBA, worked in the advertising business in Manhattan for ten years, Sydney for four, but only found home when I arrived in New Mexico. I've been blessed to have achieved many dreams, including owning a horse ranch in a spectacular place, owning my own business, and writing and publishing "Listening With My Eyes," a memoir. I am honoured to be included in this anthology and to be a member of Southwest Writers.

Rosario's Tears by Amara Cudney

Amara Cudney has had a varied and exciting career as an herbalist, retail store owner, elementary school and English as a Second Language (ESL) teacher, and author. Born in El Paso, Texas, she spent much of her life in the Southwestern United States and traveling the world, prior to moving to Hawai'i where she now lives with her husband, two dogs, a cat, and uncountable geckos. Her fiction focuses primarily on relationships and character. Her non-fiction draws heavily from her experience as an herbalist and retailer and includes a broad constellation of topics including self-improvement and home remedies, as well as her poetry which is edgy and introspective. She has a Master's Degree in Language and Literacy from the University of New Mexico. Several of her short stories and books are available from Amazon.

Forever Love by Donald DeNoon

Don, native of Indiana, was a United Methodist minister in Indiana, Missouri and Nevada before retiring in New Mexico. He is an award winning poet whose work has appeared in local news and magazine publications as well as these anthologies: SouthWest Writers--*The Storyteller's Anthology, Adobe Walls No. 5, Fixed and Free 2015 and the soon to be released Fixed and Free 2018.*

Light Transition by Mary Dorsey

I am a retired RN who worked for the public schools for over 25 years. I am also a two time cancer survivor--AML leukemia and the recipient of an experimental type of transplant (no donor needed) that saved my life. I love animals and have domesticated a colony of feral cats that give unconditional love and were a big part of my successful recovery--one always needs a reason to get out of bed in the morning--some loving living creature that needs your attention. I've been writing for as long as I can remember-and have, as yet, an unpublished novel, and children's books along with poetry that has appeared in a number of newsletters. My poetry style is eclectic: short, long, rhyming, prose, poignant, funny any subject or style that strikes my fancy at that moment. I live in near downtown Albuquerque with my fur babies. I also walk each morning and take hula lessons. Keep the mind and body in good shape. Hopefully!

Scents and Promises by Lisa Durkin

For thirty years, Lisa Durkin has been a high school science teacher with an affinity for little white dogs. She is a graduate from New Mexico Tech University with a Masters in Science Teaching. She writes education related articles for *The Beacon*, a Coalition for Excellence in Science Education quarterly publication. Her guest lecture appearances include: "Giving Your Child the Voice of Reason at School" for The Humanist Society of New Mexico.

Razzle Frazzle by Colin Patrick Ennen

Generally unimpressed with the world as it is, Colin Patrick Ennen writes satire and speculative fiction and spends far too much time in his own head. His stories have been published in The Coil, Writers Resist, and in two small press anthologies. He works as a doggie daycare supervisor and may, in fact, be part canine. Find him on Twitter @cpennen.

First Line by Roger Floyd

Roger Floyd is a retired PhD medical researcher who spent over forty years working with viruses and bacteria. He's now committed to writing full-time on science fiction novels and literary short stories. He's completed three sci-fi novels and is currently looking for a publisher. He also writes an online blog about science, writing, and the environment at rogerfloyd.wordpress.com.

The Independent Full Service Publisher by Marty Gerber

Marty Gerber had a long career as a newspaper reporter, editor, manager, and owner before segueing into publishing seven years ago as co-founder of Terra Nova Books. When not chained to his computer, he mostly stays busy dancing, playing tennis, and rock climbing, and has recently begun a wonderfully happy relationship with the guitar.

On Foot Through the Country of Painter Franticek Moric Nagl *by* Monika Ghattas

I finished raising a family, helping my husband in his business, and pursuing a teaching career. Now I am ready to do some writing and reading. I have published a book and some professional articles, but that was part of my academic career. This is the beginning of a new direction that includes a memoir that I am hoping to complete.

Exquisite Corpse group poetry by Gail Hamlin

Gail Hamlin is an author, associate publisher, and editor of over 30 reference books pertaining to Native Americans and U.S. history (published under Gail Hamlin-Wilson). She recently published "Prophetic Utterances – The Cry of His Heart (Volume 1) and Volume 2 will follow. She also enjoys writing poetry. Gail is the mother of four children and two grandchildren. She lives in Albuquerque, New Mexico.

Unrequited by Audrey Hansen

Audrey Hansen spent 14 years in advertising and writing broadcast news. Earned M.A. at University of Wisconsin, and taught at Western Illinois and Univ. of Wisconsin--Oshkosh. Also lived six years on small Colorado ranch, which became the topic of my memoir, "Coyotes Always Howl at Midnight." Moved to ABQ, held various jobs, and wrote features and news for newsletters and newspapers. Five years ago came to Oregon to be near son Chris.

Suspense Builders by Kirt Hickman

Kirt is the author of the award-winning science-fiction thrillers *Worlds Asunder* and *Venus Rain*, and was a technical writer for fourteen years before branching into fiction. His methodical approach to self-editing has helped many make sense of the mass of advice available to the novice writer. Kirt teaches self-editing classes through SouthWest Writers and has mentored several SWW members. He has spoken at numerous conferences, and contributes a monthly column titled "Revising Fiction" to the SouthWest Sage. He has also written *Mercury Sun*, the fantasy novel *Fabler's Legend*, and two children's books. His writer's guide, *Revising Fiction—Making Sense of the Madness* won a New Mexico Book award and was a finalist in the international Ben Franklin Awards.

Ginger MacGregor by Molly McGinnis Houston

Molly is a retired science and math teacher who has always loved to read. Currently she is working on two major projects: a family history and childhood memoir for her two children and their families, and a novel set in a public high school. In 2016 she won first place in an essay contest sponsored by the Albuquerque Genealogical Society. She has also written a number of short stories and for six years produced an annual newsletter for a local University of New Mexico sorority alumnae group. Virtually a lifetime resident of Albuquerque, she and her husband now live on the city's Westside.

Sometimes I Need the Distance by Arlene Hoyt-Schulze

Arlene Hoyt-Schulze was born in Neubrucke, Germany, while her father was stationed overseas in the USAF. She began writing poetry in high school and obtained her BSE in English from MSSU in Joplin, MO. She is currently working on her first novel, and refers to herself as a Nostalgic Revisionist. A collector of rocks, words, dreams and memories, she likes to travel and experiment with different art media, currently pastels.

Gray by Dennis Kastendiek

I was born and raised on the south side of Chicago, where I learned many things. For instance, desks in catholic grammar schools were actually miniature bomb shelters. In high school, I learned that the golden rectangle was the most pleasing of all geometric shapes. Then in college, I learned that much of what I knew was bullshit. I tried teaching for a while, hoping to unravel some of those thought knots for others sooner than happened for me. I'm still at it, carrying on a SWW course started by Rob Spiegal and Larry Greenly.

Niche Markets   by Rose Marie Kern

My profession was air traffic control, my vocation is writing, my avocation is self-reliant living, and my hobby is gardening. The breadth of my interests has made me a "Jill of all trades", which is how I came to write books in three genres and over 500 magazine articles. As Robert Heinlein wrote, "specialization is for insects." Currently I serve on the board of directors for SouthWest Writers and love working with new authors. My husband and I make our home south of Albuquerque near Isleta where I keep bees and have a dorky, loveable German Shephard.

The Scotsman's Wife   by Sally Kimball

Sally Kimball's stories have appeared in several anthologies: CHOICES; THE CWC LITERARY REVIEW; 2015 Anthology Voices of the Valley: Word for Word; 2016 Anthology SPARKS; and 2017 Anthology, BEYOND THE WINDOW. She was Managing Editor for the 2016 Las Positas College Anthology, BEYOND THE WINDOW. Sally is a Ministerial Counselor. She finds her inspirations through her work in the ministry and her years in the field of law enforcement. She lives in Bernalillo, New Mexico.

Benefit from Sending Emails on Long Trips   by Carol Kreis

Giant sunflowers make me smile. My professional activities indicate a restlessness, sort of like sunflower heads following the sun. I taught pre-school through college levels. I was the promotions coordinator at the zoo, co-director for the Rio Grande Writing Project for teachers, and manager of Newspapers in Education for the Albuquerque Journal and The Tribune. I developed educational materials for the Newsweek Education Program. Now I am writing a travel book with advice for seniors, based on the around-the-world trip my husband and I took for five months. At home I like watching sunflowers grow.

High Desert   by Gayle Lauradunn

Gayle Lauradunn's *Reaching for Air* was named Finalist by the Texas Institute of Letters for Best First Book of Poetry. The manuscript for her second book *All the Wild and Holy: A Life of Eunice Williams, 1696-1785* was awarded Honorable Mention by Bauhan Publishing for the May Sarton Poetry Prize and is published by Foothills Publishing. A pocket-size chapbook *Duncan Canal, Alaska* is available from Grandma Moses Press. She served on the selection committees for Albuquerque's first two Poet Laureates, and for two years chaired the Albuquerque chapter of the New Mexico State Poetry Society. While living in Amherst, MA she was the co-organizer of the First National Women's Multicultural Poetry Festival.

Last Night in the Kalihari   by Nathan McKenzie

Nathan McKenzie is a speaker by trade, a reader by chance, and a writer by heart. Born and raised in the warm Albuquerque sun, he has also lived at various times and in various seasons in Texas, California, Washington D.C., The U.K., and East Africa. Rio Rancho is where he now calls home. This marks his debut entry into the *Sage*, with hopes for many more!

Trixie's First Day   by R J Mirabal

RJ Mirabal has lived in the Middle Rio Grande Valley for most of his life. Recognized with awards for his teaching, he is now retired, pursues writing and music while volunteering with various organizations. All three books of his New Mexico-based <u>Rio Grande Parallax</u> series were Finalists in the New Mexico/Arizona Book Awards in the Fantasy/Science Fiction category. He is now working on a series of true and fantasy dog stories for ages 6–106. **Website/Blog:** <u>https://rjmirabal.wordpress.com/</u>

Minute, Writing Class   by Raymond C. Mock

Born in Denver, Colorado, mid-1950, Raymond grew up in Albuquerque, New Mexico beginning in late 1950. An electronic technician by trade, he has written poetry since the 1980s. He has published one poem, "A Smile," in *The Promise of Tomorrow* by The National Library of Poetry in 1997 and again that year by the same publisher in *A Celebration of Poets: Showcase Edition.*

Four of his poems, "Sunday Late," "Albuquerque Autumn," "Silent Din," and "Falling in Love," were published in *Muse with Blue Apples, an anthology of the New Mexico Poetry Alliance,* by Mercury HeartLink. His own book of poems and prose poems, *A Tried Heart,* was published by Mercury HeartLink in 2017.

Desert Dangers
by Elaine Carson Montague and Gary Ted Montague

The Montagues have been a team for 60 years. During 31 years with the Albuquerque Public Schools, she taught, conducted teacher training in computers and innovative programs, and earned an administrative certificate. Her real claim to fame was twelve years as The Egg Drop Lady. Gary earned a BA in Secondary Education and retired from Sandia National Laboratories after 32 years of service despite having lifelong low vision. He worked in the areas of education, training, and safety engineering. They tell of his struggle, optimism, and success in the creative nonfiction memoir, "Victory from the Shadows--Firsthand Account--Life in a School for the Blind and Beyond," ABQ Press, publisher. The book's theme is, "Persevere with integrity whatever the challenge."

Mojave Mind by Sam Moorman

After a Creative Writing M.A. at San Francisco State I worked as a home improvements contractor in Pennsylvania and California. I began full time writing only in retirement, and am on the Board of SouthWest Writers.

Night Ride by S.A. Montoya Gallegos

S.A. was born in New Mexico, but her mind, they say, has always wandered. Somehow, her stories engaged her teachers at an early age, and with their encouragement, she worked her way through life reporting reality, working in reality, and now at last she's creating a world of "reality" through her characters. S.A. finds the southwest and New Mexico truly enchanting, loves travel, gardening and exploring the "why" of people, places and things, mentally holding each up like a prism in the light.

The New Ozymandias by Connie Morgan

For thirty years, I wrote briefs and appeals for judges and juries. Now, I'd like to write poetry and prose to please myself and anyone else who might wander by. Soon, my husband and I will leave New Mexico on a quest to find America. "You, road I enter upon and look around, I believe you are not all that is here, I believe that much unseen is also here." (Walt Whitman) I'll be taking my Southwest Writers membership with me.

Her Revenge by Yoko Nagamune 長宗洋子

I was born and raised in Japan. After the 2011 mega earthquake and radiation leaks my daughter and I evacuated to Albuquerque to join my son. Here I encountered poetry and wrote a poem for the first time. The form of poetry suited me. It is short, and is less inhibiting to my limited English. I now enjoy the subtle balance of black letters and blank space on a white page.

The Slippery Slope by Evelyn M. Neil

Evelyn Neil grew up on a dairy farm in a small community in Wyoming where she acquired a lifelong affection for animals, wildflowers, western landscapes and expansive skies. She received her BS in business education and accounting from the University of New Mexico.

Evelyn served on the Board of Directors for People Living With Cancer and The Albuquerque Guild of the Santa Fe Opera. For forty years she directed the financial affairs of Kachina Petroleum Equipment Co co-founded with her husband, Don. An avid gardener, Evelyn always wanted to write but only recently found time to indulge in this passion. The people, animals and places of the past show up in her stories as well as the quail, bobcats, deer, and bears she observes around her home in the Sandia foothills.

Ambiguous Welcome by Mary Therese Padberg (Ellingwood)
My writing journey began back in middle school when the librarian invited me to join two groups: the readers club and the writers club. Since then my passion for both reading and writing have been constants in my life. Although I chose a career in mathematics, my imagination never rests and I find myself filling empty pages with a mixture of fantastical adventures and mini memoirs. Currently, I am a member of SouthWest Writers and the campus writers group at CNM where I am a mathematics professor.

Twelve Days in April by Laney Payne
Laney Payne is the pen name of Su-Ellen Lierz who has been a member of SouthWest Writers (SWW) for over five years and serves on the SWW Board. She's also a member of Women's Fiction Writers Association, as well as a critique group called "Wild Writer."

She writes speculative fiction, short-story fiction, and personal essays. In 2017, she was a finalist in the short fiction contest at the Albuquerque Museum Author Festival. As time permits, she attends writing classes through SWW and The Osher Lifelong Learning Institute (OLLI). When not working or taking classes, she enjoys being with her family and friends, and traveling with her husband, Dennis. Currently, she works for a research and development laboratory and resides in Albuquerque, New Mexico.

First Fish by Dr. Richard Peck

Richard Peck has been a New Mexican since 1990, when he became the President of UNM. Now "retired" from honest work, he writes: 29 published books, among them 9 novels, and more than 70 short stories. Over 60 productions of his 19 plays have appeared in theaters from NY to HI. Four of his short plays were recently presented in Albuquerque, and three are currently (October) playing in Ruidoso. More underway.

Life's Blueprint by Avi Shama

Avraham (Avi) Shama is a writer and a retired university professor based in Albuquerque, New Mexico. His memoir was published by Create Space, and his short pieces have appeared in the Santa Fe Literary Review, The Wall Street Journal, and in the international edition of the Jerusalem Post. He is a proud member of the Southwest Writers.

To Write Better, Draw Badly by Kathy Louise Shuit

I often think of life as a series (and sometimes a pile) of jigsaw puzzles. You try your best to fit all the pieces together and, if you keep at it, you eventually get to see the whole picture. Then, you move on to the next puzzle(s). The solving of early puzzles taught me how to serve others, a useful talent for an innkeeper and restaurateur. My grown children, grandchildren and husband of 41 years are each their own puzzle with pieces that sometimes get mixed up together and have to be sorted. The puzzle of writing is coming along; I've worked on it my whole life and sometimes wonder if I haven't lost some pieces to that one under the rug. My newest puzzle that of illustrating books for young children is just getting assembled at the corners but I think it will be beautiful when it's done. Some people say that I lack focus, I just say that I can't resist a new puzzle.

Blogging for Success by Robert Spiegel

Rob Spiegel is an award-winning journalist employed as a senior editor at Design News, an international trade magazine. He began blogging in 1998. He has blogged for a half-dozen national magazines over the years. He currently blogs for Design News as well a writing a personal blog on spirituality. He teaches blogging through the Osher program at UNM Continuing Education. He is also a journalist who also writes fiction, poetry, and drama. His work has appeared in such diverse publications as Gargoyle and Innisfree Poetry Journal, as well as Rolling Stone and True Confessions. He is a past president and current member of the SWW board of directors.

The Lantern **by Harule Stokes**

Growing up in Crown Heights, Brooklyn NY, **Harule Stokes** has seen his share of violence and drug abuse. But, armed with the knowledge of his elders, a faithful father and a strong spiritual base, Harule was able to make his way out of an assuredly dark existence and into a life of positive possibilities.

Today, married to his wonderful wife and supported by close friends, Harule is not only able to draw upon his past but to also add a new way of thinking that's both positive and uplifting. What you'll find in his work, is a wonderfully vibrant reflection of the beauty and tragedy of his youth.

SWIMMING: Cheaper Than Therapy **by Annette Thies**

I had three professions, Registered Health Information Technician, Project Management, Specialist and Co-Owner of a consulting business before I became a swim coach and realized that coaching and teaching swimming is my true passion. I joined Southwest Writers to gain insight and ideas for how to use the letters I've written to my son since he was born. I'm pleased to say I've gotten many good ideas from members and from the monthly programs and workshops I've attended. And, after two years writing has become a daily part of my life.

Just a Little Too Perfect **by Don Travis**

Don Travis is an Okie turned New Mexican. Each of his B. J. Vinson mystery novels features some region of his beautiful adopted state as prominently as it does his protagonist, a gay former Marine, ex-cop turned confidential investigator.

Don never made it to the Marines (three years in the Army instead) and certainly didn't join the Albuquerque Police Department. He thought he was a paint artist for a while but ditched that for writing a few years back. A loner, he fulfills his social needs by attending SouthWest Writers meetings and teaching a free weekly writing class called Wordwrights at the North Domingo Multigenerational Center, an Albuquerque community center. Web site: dontravis.com

Tornado Cookies by Jasmine Tritten

Jasmine Tritten is an artist, writer and world traveler born in Denmark. In 1964 she immigrated to the U.S.A. She has been journaling since childhood. Jasmine has written numerous shortstories during the last five years. *Kato's Grand Adventure*, a children's story she illustrated and wrote with her husband, was published in July 2018. *Her* memoir, *The Journey of an Adventuresome Dane*, was published in 2015 and won an award. She resides in enchanting Corrales, New Mexico with her husband and five cats. http://www.amazon.com/-/e/B00RI7ZIU0

Taking off the Uniform by Jim Tritten

Jim Tritten lives in Corrales with his Danish author-artist wife and five cats. His piece, "Taking Off the Uniform" earned him the Gold Medal winner in the category of Personal Experience – Patriotic in the 2018 National Veterans Creative Arts Festival. Jim has won thirty-four national or regional writing awards including the Alfred Thayer Mahan Award from the Navy League of the United States. He has published six books, forty-five chapters, and two hundred eighty articles, essays, etc.

Subarus are Delicious by Patricia Walkow

Patricia Walkow is an award-winning author of short stories as well as newspaper and magazine articles. A recent biography, *The War Within, the Story of Josef,* won both national and international competitions. Her work has been published in at least a dozen anthologies, both online and in print. She is a member of the Corrales Writing Group and former editor of *Corrales MainStreet News.* She resides in Corrales, New Mexico with her husband, two cats, and a dog, She enjoys traveling, gardening, tending to her koi pond, and, of course, writing.

I'm Building a Wall by Dan Wetmore

Dan Wetmore enjoys hiking, genealogy, auto mechanicing, and putting words to paper. Personal prides include having replaced an automatic transmission in field conditions in January with an extreme minimum of tools and the conflicting guidance of multiple chickens, having been allowed to remain on stage through the entire ten-minute version of "American Pie" on a karaoke dare, having employed the phrase "a palindrome of palimpsests" in a not altogether nonsensical way, and having once consumed an entire loaf of buttered toast for supper (in his prime). A transplanted North Carolinian, he's still adjusting to desert life, but revels in the distinction of living in a locale where he's able to use an 'x', two 'q's and two 'u's in daily correspondence. The family's turtle having recently been emancipated on grounds of political oppression, their cat is now feeling the increased pressures of being a single pet and is considering similar action.

An Author's Guide to Comicons by Zachry Wheeler

Zachry Wheeler is a science fiction novelist, coffee slayer, and swaggering nerd. He is based in Toronto, Ontario where he is known to lurk around museums and brewpubs. His breakout novel *Transient* is currently in development to become a feature film. Learn more at ZachryWheeler.com.

School Daze(s) by Linda Yen

Linda Yen immigrated to the United States at the age of nine. After winning a Hopwood prize for poetry at the University of Michigan, she continued to write poetry while practicing law. Her poems have appeared in the *New York Quarterly*, *Pearl*, *Northeast*, the "Walls" and "Survival" volumes of the *Poets Speak* series, and other publications. *School Daze(s)* is her first published memoir piece.

If you enjoyed this book, there are new articles and stories in the *SouthWest Sage* available free of charge each month on the SWW website!

www.southwestwriters.com

SouthWest Sage

The Voice of SouthWest Writers

Volume 34, No 8

August 2018

Contents

SWW members are invited to submit articles and information to the *Sage* and to the SWW website. Acceptance and printing is at the discretion of the editor. Contact Rose Kern at swwsage@swcp.com with proposals for new articles.

Sage Anthology Has Plethora of Choices!

This issue of the *SWW Sage* contains the final stories and articles which will be considered for inclusion in the *2018 Sage Anthology*.

Over the past three years we have received over 100 poems, stories, articles and essays which are under review for inclusion. Being published in the previous Sage newsletters means that each has already passed one review process, now our committee is reading through all of them to determine the best pieces.

No individual will have more than one piece in the Sage Anthology. There were a few poems written by groups during SWW workshops which may be allowed even if one of the group members has another piece included.

Once the selection process is complete, those individuals whose work has been selected will be contacted and asked to provide a short bio and headshot. The photo is optional, or the author can choose to substitute another type of artwork to accompany the piece. Also, the author must sign and return the form giving SWW permission to publish their work.

All funds generated by the 2018 Sage Anthology will go to SouthWest Writers. No payment other than bragging rights will accrue to the individual authors.

SouthWestWriters.com *

Made in the USA
San Bernardino, CA
12 November 2018